CLASSICAL ARAMAIC

(Assyrian - Chaldean)

ELEMENTARY BOOK 1

Classical Aramaic: Elementary Book I

ܐܘܠܦܢܐ ܕܠܫܢܐ ܐܪܡܝܐ

© 1989, 1992 by Rocco A Errico and Michael J. Bazzi

© 2015 by Rocco A. Errico and Michael J. Bazzi

Edited by Michael J. Bazzi, Rocco A. Errico, and Roy M. Gessford

ISBN: 978-1-941464-34-2

PCCN: Library of Congress Control Number: 2015957644

All Rights Reserved. Printed in the United States of America. No part of this book may be used or reproduced in any manner whatsoever without written permission except in the case of brief quotations embodied in critical articles and reviews.

PUBLISHED BY

This 2022 revised edition of *Classical Aramaic* is published by arrangement with the Noohra Foundation, Bazzi Publishing, and Let in the Light Publishing.

Cover photo credit: *Bernadit Seman. Babylon, Iraq.*
The Lion of Chaldea which represents victory over the oppressor and defender of the defenseless.

www.letinthelightpublishing.com

CONTENTS

A Word from Dr. Errico..Page v

Preface: The Aramaic Language.......................................Page vi

   1- The Aramaic Alphabet ....Page 1

Twenty Two Consonants, Seven Vowels, Numbers, Estrangela Alphabet. The Origin of the Estrangela Alphabet. Aramaic Alphabets. Vocabulary.

   2- General Basic Rules ....Page 72

Vocal Placement of Letters. Letters which do not join. Weak letters, BDOL Letters. The six Estrangela Letters, Vowels, Doubling, Plural Points, Point of Distinction. Vocalizer, Hastener, Suppressor. Occulted Letters. Accents. Syllables, Hard and Soft Letters. Punctuation. Cardinal and Ordinal Numbers.

   3- Nouns and Adjectives ....Page 94

Gender, Number, State, Vocabulary.

   4- Inseparable Prepositions ....Page 106

Rules for Prefixes – Maplatha. Vocalized and Non-Vocalized. Vocabulary.

   5- Personal Pronouns and Pronominal Suffixes ....Page 113

Subject Pronouns, Nouns with Suffixes. Pronominal Suffixes with Singular and Plural Nouns Vocabulary.

   6- Demonstrative and Interrogative Pronouns ....Page 123

Near and Distant Demonstrative Pronouns. Rules for Interrogative Pronouns Vocabulary.

   7- Verbs - An Introduction ....Page 132

The Verb. Bilateral and Quadrilateral Verbs. Active Voice. Gender, Number, Person, Moods, Tenses, Defective (indeclinable) Verbs. Past, Present and Future Conjugations. Vocabulary. The Lord's Prayer. The Beatitudes.

Vocabulary

Aramaic – English ....Page 168

English – Aramaic ....Page 182

About the Authors ....Page 195

A WORD FROM DR. ERRICO

In 1985 I became acquainted with The Rev. Fr. Michael J. Bazzi, a native Chaldean who is fluent in Aramaic (ancient and modem), Arabic, English, and Italian. We discovered that we have the same objectives concerning the need for an Eastern Aramaic grammar. My colleague, Fr. Michael, and I through a mutual work of love have created this Elementary Classical Aramaic Grammar, Book I, for English speaking people in a simple, self-teachable format. The first fruits of our labor have come to fruition.

This Elementary Aramaic Grammar, as its title implies, is a basic text and as such is meant to acquaint the student with the essentials of Aramaic. This grammar, then, does not contain all the details of a complete reference work. However, the inclusion or omission of certain grammar points have been carefully weighed by my colleague and me, and nothing which truly belongs in a beginner's book, we feel, has been omitted.

I began teaching the Aramaic approach to Scripture in 1962 and from that time. I became increasingly aware of the tremendous need for a Classical Aramaic grammar based on the Eastern alphabet for English speaking people. The Eastern (Assyrian - Chaldean) alphabet, upon which the Grammar is based, is almost identical to the ancient form of the Aramaic letters known as Estrangela. In fact, there are only six Estrangela letters which differ in shape from Eastern Aramaic (See Chapter I, p. 2 - Two forms of letters).The majority of present - day grammars taught in universities, colleges, and seminaries are based on western (Syriac) Aramaic. These grammars are detailed reference grammars mostly used by specialists in Semitic languages.

In this updated edition, Fr. Michael and I have made collections and additions after teaching with the textbook for over 20 years. We are happy to report that the majority of updates to Classical Aramaic were minor, but any changes to our teaching of Aramaic is significant. We feel this new edition will further enhance the student's ability to study and learn Classical Aramaic.

March 2022

Dr. Rocco Errico

THE ARAMAIC LANGUAGE

ܠܸܫܵܢܵܐ ܐܵܪܵܡܵܝܵܐ

Aramaic was the language of Semitic peoples throughout the ancient Near East. It was the language of the Assyrians, Chaldeans, Hebrews and Syrians. Aram and Israel had a common ancestry and the Hebrew patriarchs who were of Aramaic origin maintained ties of marriage with the tribes of Aram. The Hebrew patriarchs preserved their Aramaic names and spoke in Aramaic.

The term Aramaic ܐܵܪܵܡܵܝܵܐ is derived from Aram ܐܵܪܵܡ the fifth son of Shem, the firstborn of Noah. See Gen. 10:22. The descendants of Aram dwelt in the fertile valley, Padan-aram. The Aramaic language in Padan-aram remained pure, and in the course of time, became the common language (lingua - franca), of all the Semitic clans. By the 8th century B.C., it was the major language from Egypt to Asia Minor to Pakistan. It was employed by the great Semitic empires, Assyria and Babylon. The Persian government used Aramaic in their Western provinces.

The language of the people of Palestine shifted from Hebrew to Aramaic sometime between 721-500 B.C. Therefore, we know that Jesus, his disciples and contemporaries spoke and wrote in Aramaic. The message of Christianity spread throughout Palestine, Syria and Mesopotamia in this Semitic tongue.

Present-day scholars claim that the Aramaic language itself passed through many stages of development.

Old Aramaic	975-700 B.C
Standard Aramaic	700-200 B.C
Middle Aramaic	200 B.C – 200 A.D
Late Aramaic	200 – 700 A.D

Which includes: -

A – Western Aramaic

The Dialect of the Jews (Jerusalem, the Talmud and the Targums) and the Syro-Palestine dialect.

B – Eastern Aramaic

The Dialect of Syriac Form, Assyrian Chaldean Form, Babylon, Talmudic Aramaic and Mundaie.

Use of the Aramaic language had become common by the period of the Chaldean Empire (626-539 B.C). It became the official language of the Imperial government in Mesopotamia and enjoyed general use until the spread of Greek (331 B.C). Although Greek had spread throughout these Eastern lands. Aramaic remained dominant and the lingua franca of the Semitic peoples. This continued to be so until Aramaic was superseded by a sister Semitic tongue, Arabic, about the 13th century A.D to the 14th century A.D., when Arabic supplanted Aramaic after the Arab conquest in the 7th Century. However, the Christians of Mesopotamia (Iraq), Iran, Syria, Turkey, and Lebanon kept the Aramaic language alive domestically, scholastically and liturgically. In spite of the pressure of the ruling Arabs to speak Arabic, Aramaic is still spoken today in its many dialects, especially among the Chaldeans and Assyrians.

Before concluding, one more vital aspect of the Aramaic language needs to be mentioned and that is its use as the major Semitic tongue for the birth and spread of spiritual and intellectual ideas in and all over the Near East. According to the research and opinion of outstanding Aramaic and Arabic scholar, Professor Franz Rosenthal, "In my view, the history of Aramaic represents the purest triumph of the human spirit as embodied in language (which is the mind's most direct form of physical expression) over the crude display of material power. . . Great empires were conquered by the Aramaic language, and when they disappeared and were submerged in the flow of history, that language persisted and continued to live a life of its own . . . The language continued to be powerfully active in the promulgation of spiritual matters. It was the main instrument for the formulation of religious ideas in the Near East, which then spread in all directions all over the world . . . The monotheistic groups continue to live on today with a religious heritage, much of which found first expression in Aramaic." (F. Rosenthal, "Aramaic Studies During the Past Thirty Years," *The Journal of Near Eastern Studies*, pp.81-82, Chicago: 1978).

The Authors

CHAPTER ONE

THE ARAMAIC ALPHABET

CHAPTER ONE

THE ARAMAIC ALPHABET

There are 22 letters (Consonants) in the Aramaic alphabet. (See P. 55, 58) The letters (ܐܬܘܬܐ - Athwatha) are written from right to left. The 22 letters are usually divided into six groups: A B G D (Abgad), H W Z (Hawaz), H T Y (Haty), K L M N (Kulman), S A P S (Sapass), Q R SH T (Qarshut). Vowels are added to the consonants by using points (dots). The vowels are taught in Units two and three of Chapter One.

ܐܘܬܐ ܕܠܫܢܐ ܐܪܡܝܐ ܝܗܒܝ ܘܓܕܝܢ ܙܒܢ ܘܡܬܟܬܒܢ ܐܟ ܓ: ܐܒܓܕ، ܗܘܙ، ܚܛܝ، ܟܠܡܢ، ܣܥܦܨ، ܩܪܫܬ .

UNIT ONE

The First Group of letters:

A B G D (Abgad)

THE FIRST LETTER   ALAP   ܐܠܦ   ܐ - A

Alap is equivalent to the English letter A. It is silent and needs a vowel for vocalization. Its sound is guttural and it is known as a weak letter. (See Chapter 2, rules 1: a and 3). The numerical value of Alap is 1. The letter Alap is written in the following manner: ܐ

A- Begin at the right side of the page. Make a short horizontal line from right to left.

B- Make a small dot above the horizontal line slightly left of center.

1

C- Make a slightly slanted downward stroke from the dot to the left side of the horizontal line.

D- Write the letter Alap ܐ , ten times.

There are two forms of script (letters) used by Eastern Aramaic writers: Common writing (small letters) and Estrangela (big letters). Estrangela ܐܣܛܪܢܓܠܐ is the ancient form of the letters and was employed by scribes in writing the Gospel before classical Aramaic came into use. Thus, it derived its name Estrangela, a compound noun, from two Aramaic words: ܣܛܪ , "to write" and ܐܘܢܓܠܝܘܢ , "gospel". There are only six letters. The six letters which differ are taught in this grammar. The letter Alap in Estrangela is written in the following manner:

A- Begin at the right side of the page. Make a downward slanted stroke to the left just short of touching the base line.

B- Begin a short slanted line from the left of the previous stroke to the right.

C- Make another short slanted parallel line next to the first one connected to the upper line.

D- Write the letter Alap ܐ , A in Estrangela ten times

Alap never connects to any letter which follows it. Remember, letters always follows to the left. Examples: ܐܠܗܐ - God. (See Ch. 2, rule 2: The 8 Unjointed Letters). When Alap is a medial letter, it is joined on the right side only.

THE LETTER BETH ܒܝܬ - B

Beth is equivalent to the English letter B. It also functions as a preposition to indicate: in, by, with, through. (A preposition is a word that shows certain relations between other words. See Ch. 2, rule 4). Beth has a labial sound. (See Ch. 2, rule 1: e). When a dot is placed beneath the beth ܒ, it becomes aspirated (soft) and it has a W sound. When a dot s placed above the letter ܒ, it has a hard B sound. The numerical value of Beth is 2. The letter Beth is written in the following manner:

A- Begin at the right of the page. Make a short vertical line in a downward stroke*.

*NOTE: When Beth is preceded by any connecting letter, the first step in forming the letter is an upward vertical stroke rather than a downward stroke. Example: This rule applies to certain other letters and a reference will be made to this rule.

B- Make a short horizontal line from the top of the vertical line moving from right to left.

C- Join a short horizontal line at the bottom of the vertical line moving from right to left. Make the bottom line slightly longer than the top horizontal line.

D- Write the letter Beth ܒ , B, ten times.

E- Write the following words five times.

3

1- August – Ab – ܐܵܒ݂   _____ _____ _____ _____ _____

2- Father – Awa – ܐܲܒ݂ܵܐ   _____ _____ _____ _____ _____

3- Abbot – Aba – ܐܲܒܵܐ   _____ _____ _____ _____ _____

NOTE: The initial letter Alap in Awa (father) ܐܲܒ݂ܵܐ is not connected to the letter Beth which follows it. When a letter is joined from both sides, usually a short line is made from the previous letter to facilitate connecting the letter which follows it – ܐܲܒ݂ܵܐ (See Ch. 2, rule 7: Exceptions)

Beth connects to any letter that follows it.

***NOTE: When it is a medial letter, it is joined on both sides except when it follows one of the 8 unjointed letters. Then it connects on the left side only. (See Ch. 2, rule 2).
Also: We will number new vocabulary words throughout the book.

THE LETTER GAMAL ܓܵܡܲܠ ܓ - G

Gamal is equivalent to the English letter G. It has a palatal sound. (See Ch. 2, rule 1:C). When a dot is placed beneath Gamal, it becomes soft as in Gh. The numerical value of Gamal is 3. The letter Gamal is written in the following manner: ܓ

A- Begin at the right side of the page. Make a long slanted downward stroke.

B- Make a short horizontal line in the center of the slanted line moving towards the left.

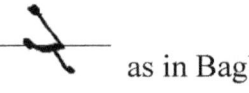

NOTE: some orthographies shape Gamal differently 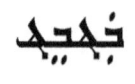 as in Bagbeg ܒܲܓ݂ܒܹܓ݂ (bubble).

4

C- Write the letter Gamal ܓ , ten times.

ܓ. ____ ____ ____ ____ ____

____ ____ ____ ____ ____

D- Write the following word five times.

4. Side – Gaba ܓܒܐ ____ ____ ____ ____

____

NOTE: ܓܒܐ is transliterated with one b – ga<u>b</u>a but it is pronounced with a double b ga<u>bb</u>a. (See Ch. 2, rule 7).

Gamal connects to any letter which follows it. When it is a medial letter, it is joined on both sides. (See **NOTE P. 4).

THE LETTER DALATH ܕܠܬ ܕ - D

Dalath is equivalent to the English letter D. It also functions as a preposition to indicate; of, from. Dalath has a lingual sound. (See Ch. 2, rule 1: b) When a dot is placed beneath ܕ it becomes soft and it has a Dh sound. The numerical value of Dalath is 4. The letter Dalath is written in the following manner: ܕ

A- Begin at the right side of the page. Make a short horizontal line.

____

B- Make a curved line moving from right to left over the short horizontal line.

ܕ

C- Make a shorter horizontal line under the first one from right to left.

ܕ

D- Write the letter Dalath ܒ݁ , D, ten times.

_____ _____ _____ _____ _____ _____ ܒ݁ .

_____ _____ _____ _____ _____ _____

E- Write the following words five times.

- 5. Bear – Diba - ܕܸܒܵܐ _____ _____ _____ _____ _____

- 6. Baghdad – ܒܲܓ݂ܕܲܕ _____ _____ _____ _____ _____

- 7. Fortune – Gada - ܓܲܕܵܐ _____ _____ _____ _____ _____

NOTE: The words diba and gada are to be pronounced as di*bb*a and ga*dd*a. (See Ch. 2, rule 7).

The letter Dalath in Estrangela is shaped differently and is written in the following manner:

ܕ

A- Begin at the right side of the page. Make a short vertical line in a downward stroke*. (See *Note: beth, p. 3).

|

B- Make a short horizontal line from right to left joined at the top of the vertical line.

ܪ

C- Place a dot in the left corner of the letter.

ܕ

D- Write the letter Dalath: ܕ D, ten times.

_____ _____ _____ _____ _____ _____

_____ _____ _____ _____ _____ _____

Dalath never connects to any letter which follows it. (See Ch. 2, rule 2). When it is a medial letter, it is joined on the right side only.

SPECIAL NOTE: When writing the Aramaic letters by hand there are seven letters which receive a fairly large dot on the top of their strokes:

1- Gamal

2- Teth ─ــݛ───

3- Lamath ─ـܠ───

4- Noon ─ـܢ───

5- Aeh ─ـܐ───

6- Yodh ─ـܝ───

7- Heth ─ـܚ───

REVIEW

1- The first four letters written in relation to each other.

ܐܒܓܕ

2- Identify the following letters by name and transliterate in the Roman (English) alphabet.

_____ ܒ _____ ܐ _____ ܓ _____ ܕ

_____ ܕ _____ ܓ _____ ܐ _____ ܒ

_____ ܕ _____ ܐ _____ ܓ _____ ܒ

_____ ܒܓܕ _____ ܐܓܕ _____ ܓܒܕ _____ ܒܓܕ _____ ܓܒܕ

Write the first four letters of the Aramaic alphabet with their English equivalent.

_____ _____

_____ _____

_____ _____

_____ _____

3- Write the Aramaic letters that correspond to the following prepositions.

Of _____ in _____ with _____

From _____ by _____ through _____

4- Write the following numbers in Aramaic.

1 _____ 2 _____ 3 _____ 4 _____

4 _____ 3 _____ 2 _____ 1 _____

5- Translate and transliterate the following words.

_____ _____ ܒܰܪܐ

_____ _____ ܓܰܒܐ

_____ _____ ܒܪ

_____ _____ ܒܓܕܕ

_____ _____ ܓܰܒܐ

_____ _____ ܒܰܪܐ

6- Write the following words in Aramaic.

August _____

Father _____

Side _____

Bear _____

Baghdad _____

Fortune _____

Abbot _____

7- Find the letter alap, beth, gamal and dalath in the following verses and circle them.

MATTHEW 5:1-2.

ܐ. ܟܕ ܚܙܐ ܕܝܢ ܝܫܘܥ ܠܟܢܫܐ ܣܠܩ ܠܛܘܪܐ ܘܟܕ ܝܬܒ ܩܪܒܘ ܠܘܬܗ ܬܠܡܝܕܘܗܝ.

ܒ. ܘܦܬܚ ܦܘܡܗ ܘܡܠܦ ܗܘܐ ܠܗܘܢ ܘܐܡܪ:

UNIT TWO

The Seven Vowels and the Second Group of Letters: -
H - W - Z (Hawaz)

THE SEVEN VOWELS

There are seven vowels in Aramaic. They are named as follows: Zqapa, Pthaha, Zlama Psheeqa, Zlama Qashya, Rwaha, Rwasa and Hwasa. In Unit Two, six of the seven vowels are to be learned.

THE FIRST VOWEL: ZQAPA

The first vowel Zqapa is an open (long) A. It is usually pronounced – ah – as in Father. Zqapa is indicated by placing two points, one above the other, directly over the letter.

Examples: - ah, - ba, - wa, -ga, - gha, - da, - dha.

NOTE: Usually when Z is the initial letter in any Aramaic word it is pronounced as a Z but in the word Zqapa it is pronounced as s, Sqapa instead of Zqapa. (See The Letter Zain, p. 16, Note– Exception to the rule).

When a word ends in an alap - and the preceding letter is vocalized with a Zqapa, the alap is indicative of that preceding vowel as in the words: side - gaba and fortune - gada. (See p. 13, Zlama Psheeqa and Zlama Qashya).

The term vocalized refer to a letter which carries a vowel - and the term unvocalized refers to a letter which does not carry a vowel –

THE SECOND VOWEL PTHAHA ܦܬ݂ܵܚܵܐ ܇

The second vowel Pthaha is a very short A as in h<u>u</u>t, <u>u</u>tter, h<u>e</u>rbal, and loc<u>a</u>l. Pthaha is indicated by placing one point over the letter and another point under it.

Examples: - ܐ݇ - uh, ܒ݇ - buh, ܓ݇ - guh, ܕ݇ - duh.

The use of uh is for sounding out the vowel but when writing (translating into English) use the letter A to indicate the Pthaha as in the words: side ܓܒܐ gaba and fortune ܓܕܐ gada.

When a letter is vocalized by a Pthaha and is followed by another vocalized letter, the second letter is doubled in pronunciation only. The letter is never doubled when written. Example: The word abbot is written ܐܒܐ with one beth ܒ , Aba, but it is pronounced as Abba. (See Ch.2, rule 7.)

We are going to learn a new letter before proceeding to the next vowel.

THE LETTER HEH ܗܹܐ ܗ - H

Heh is equivalent to the English letter H. Heh has a guttural sound. The numerical value of Heh is 5. The letter Heh is written in the following manner: ܗ

A. Begin at the right side of the page. Make a short vertical line in a downward stroke*. (See *Note: Beth, P. 3).

ㅤㅤㅤㅤㅤㅤㅤㅤㅤㅤㅤㅤㅤㅤㅤㅤㅤㅤㅤ‾‾‾‾‾‾‾‾‾
ㅤㅤㅤㅤㅤㅤㅤㅤㅤㅤㅤㅤㅤㅤㅤㅤㅤㅤㅤㅤㅤㅤ\

B. Make a short horizontal line from the top of the vertical line moving to the left completing it with a small circle in the center of the horizontal line.

ㅤㅤㅤㅤㅤㅤㅤㅤㅤㅤㅤㅤㅤㅤㅤㅤㅤㅤㅤ‾‾‾‾‾‾‾‾‾
ㅤㅤㅤㅤㅤㅤㅤㅤㅤㅤㅤㅤㅤㅤㅤㅤㅤㅤㅤㅤㅤㅤܗ

C. Write the letter Heh ܗ , H, ten times.

_____ _____ _____ _____ . ܗ

_____ _____ _____ _____ _____

D. Write the following word five times

8. One time   Gaha   ܓܵܗܵܐ _____   _____   _____   _____   _____

The letter Heh in Estrangela is shaped differently and is written in the following manner   ܗ

A. Begin at the right side of the page. Make a downward stroke* slightly curved. (See Note: beth, p. 3).

_____l_____

B. Make a short horizontal line from the top of the first stoke moving to the left.

_____┐_____

C. Make another downward stroke slightly curved to the left from the left of the horizontal line.

_____ᑕ┐_____

D. Make a vertical line in the center from the top horizontal line.

_____ᑕ╥_____

E. Write the letter Heh   ܗ H, ten times.

_____   _____   _____   _____   _____

_____   _____   _____   _____   _____

Heh is never connected to any letter which follows it. (See Ch 2, rule 2).

When it is a medial letter, it is joined on the right side only.

THE THIRD VOWEL: ZLAMA PSHEEQA   ܘܠܵܗܿܕ ܦܹܫܝܼܩܵܐ   ܐܸ

The third vowel Zlama Psheeqa is a very short I. It is pronounced as in sit and hit. Zlama Psheeqa is indicated by placing two points side by side under the letter.

Examples:- ܐ -I, ܒ -bi, ܓ -gi, ܕ -di, ܗ -hi.

When a letter is vocalized by a Zlama Psheeqa and is followed by another vocalized letter, the second letter is doubled in pronunciation only. (Exactly like the Pthaha. See Ch. 2 rule 7). The word for bear is written ܕܒܐ - diba, but it is pronounced as dibba.

REMINDER: - When a word ends in an alap - ܐ and the preceding letter is vocalized with a Zqapa ܒ, or Zlama Psheeqa ܒ, the final alap is indicative of that preceding vowel as in qri ܩܪܝ - a contraction of the word qritha ܩܪܝܬܐ - village. (See note under Zqapa, p. 10).

THE FOURTH VOWEL: ZLAMA QASHYA ܙܠܡܐ ܩܫܝܐ

The fourth vowel Zlama Qashya ia an open E. It is pronounced eh as in b<u>ear</u>, p<u>ear</u>. It is like <u>ey</u> in English they without the final I or Y glide, Zlama Qashya is indicated by placing two points in a slant, one above the other, under the letter.

Examples: - ܐ - eh, ܒ - beh, ܓ - geh, ܕ - deh, ܗ - heh. ܒܕܐ - Badeh - Fish egg.

NOTE: - When a word ends in an alap - ܐ and the preceding letter is vocalized with a Zqapa ܒ, Zlama Psheeqa ܒ, or Zlama Qashya ܒ, the final alap is indicative of the preceding vowel as in badeh ܒܕܐ. (See Note under Zqapa, p. 10 and Zlama Psheeqa above).

Aramaic speaking people teach the vowels by using certain positions of the mouth. We are going to use only four of these positions.

1- Zqapa, long and open A. Open the mouth widely as in father.
2- Pthaha, a short A. open the mouth slightly as in hot or hut.
3- Zlama Psheeqa, is a very short e. Drop the chin slightly and pronounce sit.
4- Zlama Qashya short e – eh. Drop the chin and pronounce – dare.

We are going to learn a new letter before proceeding to the next vowel.

THE LETTER WAW - ܘܐܘ ܘ - W

Waw is equivalent to the English letter W. It also functions as a conjunction to indicate and. It has a labial sound and it is known as a weak consonant. (See Ch. 2, rule 1: e and 3) The numerical value of Waw is 6. The letter Waw is written in the following manner: - ܘ

NOTE: - When the letter – waw – is set in type (printed) it is in the shape of a complete circle ܘ But when it is written by hand waw is not a complete circle: ܩ

A- Begin at the right side of the page. Make a short vertical line.

B- Begin at the top of the vertical line and make a half circle to the left.

C- Write the letter Waw ܘ , W, ten times.

D- Write the following words five times.

9. Inside   Gawa   ܓܘܐ

10. Foolish   Boda   ܒܘܕܐ

Waw never connects to any letter which follows it. (See Ch. 2, rule 2). When is a medial letter, Waw is joined on the right side only.

THE FIFTH VOWEL: RWAHA - ܪܘܵܚܵܐ   ܘ݁

The fifth vowel Rwaha is O as in oh. The Rwaha is indicated by placing a point over the letter waw ܘ = ܘ݁ and waw becomes the vowel O.

Examples: - ܘ݁ܐ - oh, ܒܘ݁ - boh, ܓܘ݁ - go, ܓ݂ܘ݁ - gho, ܕܘ݁ - doh, ܕ݂ܘ݁ - dhoh, ܗܘ݁ - ho.

Note: When the letter ܘ has a dot over or beneath it, Waw becomes a vowel. With a dot above Waw becomes ܘ݁ pronounced Rwaha; with a dot beneath Waw becomes ܘ݂ pronounced Rwasa.

THE SIXTH VOWEL: RWASA - ܪܘܵܣܵܐ   ܘ݂

The sixth vowel Rwasa is OO or U. Rwasa is indicated by placing one point under the letter waw   ܘ ܘ݂ and waw becomes the vowel OO or U as in room.

Examples: - ܘ݂ܐ - OO, ܒܘ݂ - boo, ܓܘ݂ - goo, ܓ݂ܘ݂ - ghoo, ܕܘ݂ - doo, ܕ݂ܘ݂ - dho, ܗܘ݂ - hoo.

Exercise: - Write the following words four times.

11. Wall, side   Gooda   ܓܘܼܕܵܐ   _____ _____ _____ _____

12. Well,   Gooba   ܓܘܼܒܵܐ   _____ _____ _____ _____

15

THE LETTER ZAIN ‒ ܙܝܢ ‒ Z

Zain is equivalent to the English letter Z. It has a dental sound. Dentals are also called sibilants because of their hissing sound. (See Ch. 2, rule 1: d). The numerical value of Zain is 7. The letter Zain is written in the following manner: ܙ

A- Begin at the right side of the page. Make a short downward stroke past the base line slightly curved to the left.

B- Beginning at the top of the curved line make a downward vertical stroke to the base line.

C- Write the letter Zain ܙ, Z, ten times.

D- Write the following words five times.

13. Bell   Zaga   ܙܓܐ

14. Treasure   Gaza   ܓܙܐ

NOTE: Exception to the rule. When an unvocalized Z is followed by a vocalized Kap ܟ or ܩ qop the letter Zain is pronounced as s instead of Z as in ܘܙܟܪܝܐ skharya and ܘܙܩܦܐ Sqapa.

Zain never connects to any letter which follows it. (See Ch. 2, rule 2). When it is a medial letter, it is joined on the right side only.

REVIEW

1- The Aramaic letters from ܒ - ܘ written in relation to each other.

   ܘ ܘ ܗ ܕ ܓ ܒ ܐ

2- Identify the following letters by name and transliterate in the Roman (English) alphabet.

   ܘ ܘ ܗ ܕ ܓ ܒ ܐ

   ܗ ܘ ܘ ܓ ܐ ܕ ܒ

   ܘ ܐ ܘ ܗ ܕ ܒ ܓ

3- Write the first seven letters of the Aramaic Alphabet with their English equivalents.

   _____ _____
   _____ _____
   _____ _____
   _____ _____
   _____ _____
   _____ _____
   _____ _____

4- Name the following six vowels giving an example for each vowel.

   _____ _____ ܘ݁   _____ _____ ܘ݈

   _____ _____ ܘ݂   _____ _____ ܘ݊

17

_____ _____ ܘ؛ _____ _____.ܘ́

5- Name and write the five consonants, which do not join to the letter, which follows them.

_____ _____
_____ _____
_____ _____
_____ _____
_____ _____

6- Write the following conjunction in Aramaic.

And _____

7- Write the following numbers in Aramaic.

1 _____ 2 _____ 3 _____ 4 _____
5 _____ 6 _____ 7 _____

7 _____ 6 _____ 5 _____ 4 _____
3 _____ 2 _____ 1 _____ .

8- Practice reading: The letters with their vowels.

ܿܐ ܿܒ ܿܓ ܿܕ ܿܗ ܿܘ ܿܙ ܿܚ

ܹܐ ܹܒ ܹܓ ܹܕ ܹܗ ܹܘ ܹܙ ܹܚ

ܸܐ ܸܒ ܸܓ ܸܕ ܸܗ ܸܘ ܸܙ ܸܚ

ܼܐ ܼܒ ܼܓ ܼܕ ܼܗ ܼܘ ܼܙ ܼܚ

ܘܿܐ ܘܿܒ ܘܿܓ ܘܿܕ ܘܿܗ ܘܿܙ ܘܿܚ

ܘܼܐ ܘܼܒ ܘܼܓ ܼܘܕ ܼܘܗ ܼܘܙ ܼܘܚ

19

UNIT THREE

The Final Vowel and the Third Group of Letters
H T Y (Haty)

THE LETTER HETH ܚܝܬ ܚ - H

Heth has no precise equivalent English letter. When it is pronounced, it is a hard H almost double in sound HH. This is indicated by writing an H and placing a dot beneath it H. It has a guttural sound but comes from the chest near the trachea. The numerical value of Heth is 8. The letter Heth is written in the following manner: ܚ

A- Begin at the right side of the page. Make a short curved u.

B- Finish the u with a short horizontal line on the left.

NOTE: When the letter Heth ܚ stands alone the short horizontal line ends with an upward stroke, but when it joins another letter the horizontal line is written straight so that it may connect to the next letter - ܚܘܣܬܢܐ prosperity.

C- Write the letter Heth, H, ten times.

D- Write the following words five times.

15. Brother - Aha ܐܰܚܳܐ _____ _____ _____ _____ _____

16. Love - Hubba ܚܽܘܒܳܐ _____ _____ _____ _____ _____

17. Prosperity - Buhbaha ܒܽܘܚܒܳܗܳܐ _____ _____ _____ _____

_____ _____

Heth connects to any letter, which follows it. When it is a medial letter, it is joined on both sides. (See ** NOTE, p. 4).

THE LETTER TETH ܛܶܝܬ ܛ

The letter Teth has no precise equivalent English letter. When it is pronounced it is a hard T almost double in sound TT. It is like the English name Boston. This is indicated by writing a T and placing a dot beneath it T. It has a lingual sound. The numerical value of Teth is 9. (Note that the letter A through T, ܐ — ܛ are the single figures 1 - 9). The letter Teth is written in the following manner: ܛ

A- Begin at the right side of the page. Make a medium horizontal line from right to left.

B- Begin at the right of the horizontal line and make a short downward slanted left stroke to the center of the first line.

C- Begin at the base of the slanted line and make an upward slanted stroke to the left extending above the base line.

21

D- Write the letter Teth ܛ T, ten times.

_____ _____ _____ _____ _____ _____ . ܛ

_____ _____ _____ _____ _____

E- Write the following words, five times.

18. Good - Tawa ܛܒܼܵܐ _____ _____ _____ _____ _____

19. Cook - Tabaha ܛܲܒܵܚܵܐ _____ _____ _____ _____ _____

20. Sin - Htaha ܚܛܵܗܵܐ _____ _____ _____ _____ _____

Teth connects to any letter which follows it. When it is a medial letter, it is joined on both sides. (See ** NOTE, p. 4).

THE LETTER YODH ܝܘܿܕ ܝ Y / I / E

The letter Yodh is equivalent to the English letter Y. When it functions as a vowel it is either EE or I. Its sound is Palatal and it is known as a weak consonant. (See Ch 2, rule 1:c and 3). Note that the letters alap ܐ , waw ܘ and yodh ܝ are known as the three weak consonants. They are pronounced together as : " **Oye**." The numerical value of Yodh is 10. Beginning with Yodh ܝ each succeeding letter is counted by tens until the letter Qop ܩ (100) .Thus , ܝܐ is 11 and ܝܛ is 19. In Aramaic the higher number such as 10 ܝ precedes the lesser figure 1 ܐ . Thus, it is always written as 10 and 1 = 11, ܝ and ܐ = ܝܐ . The letter yodh is written in the following manner: ܝ

A- Begin at the right side of the page. Make a short curved u.

_____
_____ ܝ

NOTE: When the letter Yodh stands alone the final end of the u ends with the upward stroke - ܝ but when it joins another letter the final end of the u is written as a horizontal line - ܝܫܘܿܥ , Jesus.

B- Write the letter Yodh, ܝ Y, ten times.

_____ _____ _____ _____ _____ _____ . ܝ

_____ _____ _____ _____ _____ _____

C- Write the following words five times.

21. Alive - Haya   ܚܲܝܵܐ   _____ _____ _____ _____ _____

22. Snake - Haywa ܚܲܝܘܵܐ   _____ _____ _____ _____ _____

23. Sinner - Hataya ܚܲܛܵܝܵܐ _____ _____ _____ _____ _____

Yodh connects to any letter which follows it. When it is a medial letter, it is joined on both sides. (See ** NOTE, p. 4).

THE FINAL VOWEL: HWASA ܒ݁ ܚܒ݂ܵܨܵܐ

The seventh and final vowel Hwasa is a long ee. It is pronounced as in the word Bee.

Hwasa is indicated by placing a point directly beneath the Yodh ܝ - ܝ݇ as in Beeba ܒܝܒܐ Canal.

Examples: - ܐܝ - ee, ܒܝ - bee, ܒܝ - wee, ܓܝ - gee, ܓ݂ܝ - ghee, ܕܝ - dee, ܕ݂ܝ - dhee, ܗܝ - hee, ܘܝ - wee, ܙܝ - zee, ܚܝ - hee, ܛܝ - tee.

NOTE: - When a letter is vocalized by a pthaha ܲ and is followed by a yodh ܝ a dipthong sound is produced - ae or ay as in the month of May.

Examples: ܒܲܝܬܵܐ - bayta, house.

23

REVIEW

1- The Aramaic letter ܒ - ܝ written in relation to each other.

_____

2- Identify the following letters by name and transliterate in the Roman (English) alphabet.

3- Write the first ten letters of the Aramaic alphabet with zqapa and pthaha.

_____   _____

_____   _____

_____   _____

_____   _____

_____   _____

_____   _____

_____   _____

_____   _____

_____   _____

_____   _____

4- Memorize the following chart.

THE SEVEN VOWELS

VOWEL	NAME	EXAMPLES
͖	ܙܩܦܐ	ܙܵܐ
̇	ܦܬܚܐ	ܟܲܬ
̤	ܘܠܡܕ ܦܣܝܩܐ	ܕܸܢ
̤	ܘܠܡܕ ܩܫܝܐ	ܬܹܘ
ܘ	ܪܘܨܐ	ܚܘܿܕ
ܘ	ܪܒܨܢܐ	ܗܘܼܕ
̤	ܚܒܨܢܐ	ܚܝܼܕ

5- Write the first ten letters of the Aramaic alphabet with Zlama Psheeqa and Zlama Qashya.

_____   _____

_____   _____

_____   _____

_____   _____

_____   _____

25

_____   _____

_____   _____

_____   _____

_____   _____

6- Write the following numbers in Aramaic.

1 _____ , 2 _____ , 3 _____ , 4 _____ , 5 _____ 6 _____ ,
7 _____ , 8 _____ , 9 _____ , 10, _____ 11 _____ , 12 _____ ,
13 _____ , 14 _____ , 15 _____ , 16 _____ , 17 _____ ,
18 _____ , 19 _____ , 20 _____ .

7- Practice reading: The letters with their vowels.

ܕܻ ܠܻ ܒܻ

ܕܷ ܠܷ ܒܷ

ܕܶ ܠܶ ܒܶ

ܕܹ ܠܹ ܒܹ

ܕܳ ܠܳ ܒܳ

ܕܽ ܠܽ ܒܽ

ܠܒܻ ܛܻ ܣܻ ܘܻ ܩܻ ܗܻ ܕܻ ܓܻ ܠܻ ܙܻ ܪܻ

8- Translate and transliterate the following words.

ܚܘܫܒܢܐ

ܣܘܦܐ

ܐܢܐ

ܣܝܦܐ

ܐܠܦܐ

ܐܒܐ

ܗܢܐ

ܚܕܐ

ܐܝܕܐ

UNIT FOUR

The Fourth Group of letters:
K L M N (Kulman)

THE LETTER KAP AND KAP ܟ݂ܟ ܘܟ݁ܟ   ܟ - K / C / Q

The letter Kap is equivalent to the English K. It has a palatal sound. When a dot is placed beneath the Kap ܟ݂ , the letter becomes soft Kh as in the German pronunciation Ch – Ba<u>ch</u>, but when the dot is placed above the letter ܟ݁ , it becomes a hard K. The numerical value of Kap is 20. Thus ܟܒ is 22 and ܟܚ is 28. (See the letter Yodh, p. 22, the higher number preceding the lesser figure).

The letter Kap ܟ has three forms of writing:

1) Initial and medial form ܟ .

2) The first final form when the preceding letter is not joined to the final Kap ܟ .

3) The second final form when the preceding letter is joined to the final Kap ܟ .

The initial and medial letter Kap is written in the following manner: ܟ

A- Begin at the right side of the page. Make a curved line moving from right to left.

B- Make a medium horizontal line from the base of the curved line.

C- Write the letter Kap ܟ , ten times.

_____ _____ _____ _____ _____ .

D- Write the following words five times.

24. Thorn - ܟܘܒܐ _____ _____ _____ _____

25. Palate Jaw - Hika ܚܟܐ _____ _____ _____ _____
_____

26. Star - Kawkwa ܟܘܟܒܐ _____ _____ _____ _____
_____.

THE FIRST FINAL FORM ܟ (Separate)

A- Begin at the right side of the page. Make a half circle from right to left.

_____ ܂

B- Make a short slanted upward stroke from the left side of the half circle.

_____ ܂

C- Make another short slanted upward stroke to the right from the slanted line.

_____ ܂

D- Make a slanted downward stroke to the left from the right side of the half circle.

(Do not go beyond the left side of the half circle).

_____ ܟ

E- Write the first final form of Kap ܟ , ten times.

_____ _____ _____ _____ _____ . ܟ

29

_____ _____ _____ _____ _____ _____ _____ .

F- Write the following word five times.

27. Place, Position, Spot Dook ܕܘܟܗ _____ _____ _____ _____

_____ .

THE SECOND FINAL FORM ܟ (JOINED)

A- Begin at the right side of the page. Make a short upward slanted line from right to left.

B- From the top of the slanted line make a short slanted downward stroke from right to left.

C- Make a long slanted downward stroke to the right from the last stroke.

D- At the end of the long slanted line make a short upward slanted stroke to the ight.

E- Write the second final form of Kap ܟ ten times.

_____ _____ _____ _____ _____ ܟ .

_____ _____ _____ _____ _____ .

F- Write the following word five times.

28. Laughed - Ghek ܓܚܟ _____ _____ _____ _____

_____ .

30

THE LETTER LAMADH ܠ - L

The letter Lamadh is equivalent to the English letter L. It also functions as a preposition to indicate: to, for. It has a lingual sound. The numerical value of Lamadh is 30. Thus  is 33 and  is 37. (See the letter Yodh – p. 22, the higher number preceding the lesser figure). The letter Lamadah is written in the following manner: - ܠ

A- Begin at the right side of the page. Begin above the base line and make a long slanted downward stroke from left to right to the base line.

B- Join a short horizontal line at the base of the slanted line from right to left. (Do not go beyond the top of the slanted line).

C- Write the letter Lamadh ܠ , L, ten times.

_____ _____ _____ _____ _____ . ܠ

_____ _____ _____ _____ _____ .

D- Write the following words five times.

29. No - La ܠܐ _____ _____ _____ _____ _____

30. Heart - Liba - ܠܒܐ _____ _____ _____ _____ _____

31. God - Alaha - ܐܠܗܐ _____ _____ _____ _____ _____

32. Wedding - Hlola ܚܠܘܠܐ _____ _____ _____ _____ _____

Note: - An exception occurs in the word ܐܠܗܐ , the Pthaha over ܐ is pronounced as Zqapa.

Lamadh connects to any letter which follows it. When it is a medial letter, it is joined on both sides.

THE LETTER MEEM AND MEEM ܡ ܡܝܡ ܘܡܝܡ - M

The letter Meem is equivalent to the English letter M. It has a labial sound. The numerical value of Meem is 40. Thus ܡܕ is 44 and ܡܘ is 46. (See the letter Yodh, p. 22, The higher number preceding the lesser figure).

The letter Meem in classical Aramaic has two forms of writing.

1) Initial and medial form ܡ܀

2) Final form which appears at the end of a word ܡ in Estrangela the final Meem is the same as the Classical Aramaic.

The initial and medial letter Meem is written in the following manner: ܡ܀

A- Begin at the right side of the page. Make a half circle from right to left.

_____ ܿ _____

B- Beginning at the left of the half circle make a very short slanted upward stroke to the left.

_____ ܿ _____

C- Make a medium horizontal stroke beginning at the right of the half circle extending beyond the short upward stroke.

_____ ܿ _____

D- Write the letter Meem ܡ , M, ten times

_____ _____ _____ _____ _____ ܡ܀

_____ _____ _____ _____ _____

E- Write the following words five times.

33. King - Malka ܡܲܠܟܵܐ _____ _____ _____ _____

34. Wise - Hakima ܚܲܟܝܼܡܵܐ _____ _____ _____ _____

THE FINAL MEEM ܡ (It remains the same shape in Estranela).

A- Begin at the right side of the page. Make a short downward vertical stroke.

_____ ܝ

B- Make a long horizontal line from the top of the vertical stroke to the left.

_____ ┐

C- Make a short horizontal line from the bottom of the vertical stroke to the left. (Do not go beyond the center of the top horizontal line).

_____ ܕ

D- From the center of the top horizontal line make a slanted medium downward stroke to the left.

_____ ܡ

E- Write the final Meem ܡ , ten times.

_____ _____ _____ _____ _____ ܡ .

_____ _____ _____ _____ _____

F- Write the following words five times.

35. Dream - Helma - ܚܸܠܡܵܐ _____ _____ _____ _____ _____

36. Adam - Adham - ܐܵܕܵܡ _____ _____ _____ _____ _____

The letter Meem ㄲ in Estrangela is written in the following manner and it is used only as an initial and medial letter. Remember the final Meem is the same in Estrangela and Classical Aramaic.

A- Begin at the right side of the page. Make a short downward vertical stroke.

˥

B- Make a long horizontal line from the top of the vertical stroke.

┐

C- Make a very short horizontal line from the downward vertical stroke to the left. (Do not go beyond the center of the top horizontal line).

┐

D- Make a short downward stroke from the center of the horizontal line finishing at the base line.

ㄲ

E- Beginning from the last stoke make a short horizontal line to the left.

ㄲ

F- Write the letter Meem ㄲ M, ten times.

___ ___ ___ ___ ___
___ ___ ___ ___ ___

Examples: King - Malka

Meem connects to any letter which follows it. When it is a medial letter, it is joined on both sides. (See ** NOTE, p. 4).

THE LETTER NOON AND NOON ܢܘܢ ܘܢܘܢ - ܢ - N

The letter Noon is equivalent to the English letter N. It has a lingual sound. The numerical value of Noon is 50. Thus, ܢܗ is 55 and ܢܛ is 59. (See the letter Yodh, p. 22, the higher number preceding the lesser figure).

The letter Noon ܢ has three forms of writing.

1) The initial and medial form ܢ

2) The first final form when the preceding letter is not joined to the final noon ܢ

3) The second final form when the preceding letter is joind to the final noon ܢ

The initial and medial letter Noon is written in the following manner: ܢ

A- Begin at the right side of the page. Make a very short vertical line in a downward stroke*. (See *Note: beth, p. 4).

_____ ܐ

B- Make a horizontal line connecting at the bottom of the short vertical line to the left.

_____ ܐ

C- Write the letter Noon ܢ , N, ten times.

_____ _____ _____ _____ _____ . ܢ

_____ _____ _____ _____ _____

D- Write the following words five times.

37. Rest - Nyaha - ܢܝܚܐ _____ _____ _____ _____ _____

35

38. Merciful - Hanana - ܡܢܢܐ _____ _____ _____ _____ _____

39. Ear - Idhna - ܐܕܢܐ _____ _____ _____ _____ _____

THE FIRST FINAL FORM ܢ (Separate)

A- Begin at the right side of the page. Make a small dot.

B- Make a medium downward stroke to the right.

C- Write the first final form of Noon ܢ , ten times.

_____ _____ _____ _____ _____

_____ _____ _____ _____ _____

D- Write the following words five times.

40. December - Kanon - ܟܢܘܢ ܐ _____ _____ _____ _____

_____

41. January - Kanon - ܟܢܘܢ ܒ _____ _____ _____ _____

_____

THE SECOND FINAL FORM ܢ ܢܢ (Joined)

A- Begin at the right side of the page. Make a short horizontal line from right to left.

B- Beginning at the left of the horizontal line make a slanted downward stroke to the right. (Do not go beyond the horizontal line).

C- Write the second final form of Noon ܢ , ten times.

_____ _____ _____ _____ _____ ܢ.

_____ _____ _____ _____ _____

D- Write the following words five times.

42. John - Yohanan - ܝܘܚܢܢ _____ _____ _____ _____ _____

43. Jonah - Yonan - ܝܘܢܢ _____ _____ _____ _____ _____

Noon connects to any letter which follows it. When it is a medial letter, it is joined on both sides. (See **NOTE, p. 4).

REVIEW

1- The Aramaic letters ܐ - ܢ written in relation to each other.

ܐܒܓܕܗܘܙܚܛܝܟܠܡܢ

2- Identify the following letters by name and transliterate in the Roman (English) alphabet.

ܐ – ܒ – ܓ‍ – ܕ – ܗ – ܘ – ܚ – ܛ –

– ܝ – ܟ – ܠ – ܡ‍ – ܢ –

ܐ – ܒ – ܓ‍ – ܘ – ܚ – ܝ – ܠ – ܢ – ܡ‍ – ܟ – ܛ –

– ܘ – ܗ – ܕ – ܐ –

ܢ – ܡ‍ – ܠ – ܟ – ܝ – ܚ – ܛ – ܘ – ܗ –

– ܕ – ܓ‍ – ܒ – ܐ –

3- Write the following number in Aramaic.

11 _____ 13 _____ 16 _____ 18 _____ 20 _____

21 _____ 22 _____ 23 _____ 24 _____ 25 _____

26 _____ 27 _____ 28 _____ 29 _____ 30 _____
35 _____ 39 _____ 40 _____ 46 _____ 49 _____
50 _____ 60 _____ 70 _____ 80 _____ 90 _____ .

4- Practice reading: The letters with their vowels.

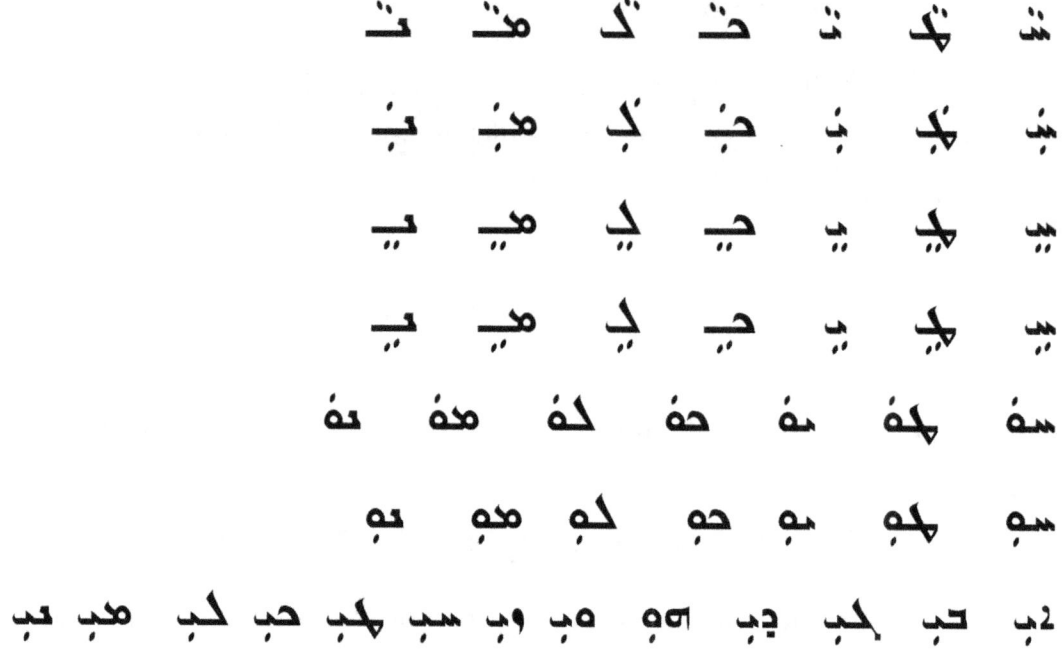

5- Translate the following English words into Aramaic words.

August _____

Side _____

Baghdad _____

Fortune _____

Fish egg _____

Father _____

Bear _____

Time _____

Den, Well _____

Inside _____

Wall _____

38

Treasure   _____

Love   _____

Good   _____

Sin   _____

Foolish   _____

Bell   _____

Brother   _____

Prosperity   _____

Cook   _____

Jonah   _____

6- Translate and transliterate the following words.

_____   _____   ܐܝܕܐ

_____   _____   ܒܝܬܐ

_____   _____   ܝܡܐ

_____   _____   ܕܗܒ

_____   _____   ܟܠ

_____   _____   ܐܟܬܒܐ

_____   _____   ܡܠܟܐ

_____   _____   ܝܠܕܐ

_____   _____   ܢܫܐ

_____   _____   ܪܘܚܐ

39

		ܐܒܗܝ 2
_____	_____	ܐܒܗܝ ܕ
_____	_____	ܒܝܬܐ
_____	_____	ܚܘܒܐ
_____	_____	ܟܘܟܒܐ
_____	_____	ܚܝܝ
_____	_____	ܠܚܡܐ
_____	_____	ܣܠܘܩܐ
_____	_____	ܫܒܝܩܐ
_____	_____	ܢܗܪ
_____	_____	ܩܘܒܬܐ

7- Find the letters ܡ - ܒ in the following verses and circle them.

MATTHEW 5:1 – 2

2 . ܟܕ ܚܙܐ ܕܝܢ ܝܫܘܥ ܠܟܢܫܐ ܣܠܩ ܠܛܘܪܐ ܘܟܕ ܝܬܒ ܩܪܒܘ ܠܘܬܗ ܬܠܡܝܕܘܗܝ .

ܒ ܘܦܬܚ ܦܘܡܗ ܘܡܠܦ ܗܘܐ ܠܗܘܢ ܘܐܡܪ:

40

UNIT FIVE

The Fifth Group of letters
S A P S (Saapas)

THE LETTER SIMKATH ܣܡܟܼܵܬܼ ܣ -S

Simkath is equivalent to the English letter S. It has a dental sound (sibilant). The numerical value of Simkath is 60. Thus, ܣܐ is 61 and ܣܚ is 68. (See the letter Yodh, p. 22, the higher number preceding the lesser figure). Simkath is written in the following manner: ܣ

A- Beginning at the right of the page. Make a short curved line upward from right to left.

B- Beginning at the bottom of the curved line make an upward stroke to the left slightly beyond the curved line.

C- Complete the upward stroke from the left to the right forming a semi-circle.

D- Make a short horizontal line fom the top center of the letter moving to the left.

NOTE: When Simkath is the final letter of a word it is written:

E- Written the letter Simkath ܣ , S, ten times.

F- Write the following words five times.

44. Thief - Gayasa - ܓܝܣܐ _____ _____ _____ _____ _____

45. Horse - Susia - ܣܘܣܝܐ _____ _____ _____ _____ _____

46. Wart - Sisa - ܣܝܣܐ _____ _____ _____ _____ _____

Simkath connects to any letter which follows it. When it is a medial letter, it is joined on both sides. (See** NOTE, p. 4).

THE LETTER AEH ܥ ܥ - A

Aeh has no precise equivalent English letter. It is pronounced like e in they without the final i or y glide. It is also like the airline Al Alia. It has a guttural sound and it is a glottal stop. The numerical value of Aeh is 70. Thus, ܥܒ is 72 and ܥܙ is 77. (See the letter Yodh, p. 22, the higher number preceding the lesser figure). The letter Aeh is written in the following manner: ܥ

A- Begin at the right side of the page. Make a very short horizontal line.

B- Beginning at the left of the horizontal line make an upward slanted medium stroke to the left.

C- Make a short horizontal line beginning at the left of the first stroke. (Don't go beyond the top of the slanted line).

D- Write the letter Aeh ܥ , A, ten times.

_____ _____ _____ _____ _____ _____ _____ ܕ.

_____ _____ _____ _____ _____ _____

E- Write the following words five times.

47. World - alma ܥܠܡܐ _____ _____ _____ _____ _____

48. Forever - Laalam ܠܥܠܡ _____ _____ _____ _____ _____

49. Eye - Ayna ܥܝܢܐ _____ _____ _____ _____ _____

50. Gust, Whirlwind, Hurricane, Twister – Alaala ܥܠܥܠܐ _____ _____

_____ _____ _____

Aeh connects to any letter which follows it. When it is a medial letter, it is joined on both sides. (See **NOTE, p. 4).

THE LETTER ܦܐ ܦ -P

Peh is equivalent to the English letter P. When a small semicircle is placed beneath the Peh, ܦ̮ , it becomes soft and has a W sound. Peh has a labial sound. The numerical value of Peh is 80. Thus, ܦܓ is 83 and ܦܚ is 88. (See the letter Yodh, p. 22, the higher number preceding the lesser figure). The letter Peh is written in the following manner: ܦ

A- Begin at the right side of the page. Make a medium slanted downward stroke* to the right. (See **NOTE: beth, p. 4).

B- Make a small half circle on the left of the slanted line close to the top.

C- Make a short horizontal line at the base of the slanted line from right to left.

43

NOTE: When Peh is not standing alone, the upward stroke is make with an immediate top circle.

ܦ

D- Write the letter Peh ܦ , P, ten times.

_____ _____ _____ _____ _____ _____ . ܦ

_____ _____ _____ _____ _____ _____

E- Write the following words five times.

51. Pope - Papa - ܦܵܦܵܐ _____ _____ _____ _____ _____

52. Teacher - Malpana - ܡܲܠܦܵܢܵܐ _____ _____ _____ _____ _____

53. Pagan – Hanpa - ܚܲܢܦܵܐ _____ _____ _____ _____ _____

54. Mouth – Pooma - ܦܘܿܡܵܐ _____ _____ _____ _____ _____

Peh connects to any letter which follows it. When it is a medial letter, it is joined on both sides. (See **NOTE, p. 4).

THE LETTER SADHE ܨܵܕܹܐ ܨ - S

Sadhe has no precise equivalent English letter. When it is pronounced, it is a double SS as in So and Sun. It has a dental sound (sibilant). The numerical value of sadhe is 90. Thus, ܨܕ is 94 and ܨܛ is 99. Sadhe is the last letter that is used for double figures – tens. (See the letter Yodh, p. 22, The higher number preceding the lesser figure). The letter Sadhe is written in the following manner: ܨ

44

A- Begin at the right side of the page. Make a short u.

B- Beginning at the left side of the u make a downward slightly curved medium stroke to the right. (Do not go beyond the beginning of the u).

C- Beginning at the end of the curve make a medium horizontal stroke to the left.

D- Write the letter Sadhe ܨ , S, ten times.

_____ _____ _____ _____ _____ . ܨ

_____ _____ _____ _____ _____

E- Write the following words five times.

55. Fast – Sauma - ܨܘܡܐ _____ _____ _____ _____ _____

56. Image, Statue, Idol - Salma ܨܠܡܐ _____ _____ _____ _____ _____

57. Harvest – Hsada - ܚܨܕܐ _____ _____ _____ _____ _____

    Sadhe never connects to any letter which follows it. (See Ch. 2, rule 2). When it is a medial letter, it is joined on the right side only.

45

REVIEW

1- The Aramaic letters 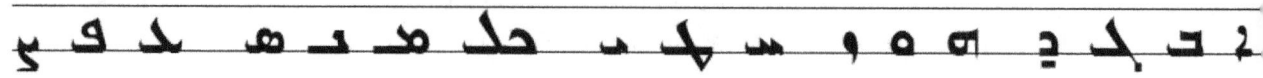 written in relation to each other.

2- Identify the following letters by name and transliterate in the Roman (English) alphabet.

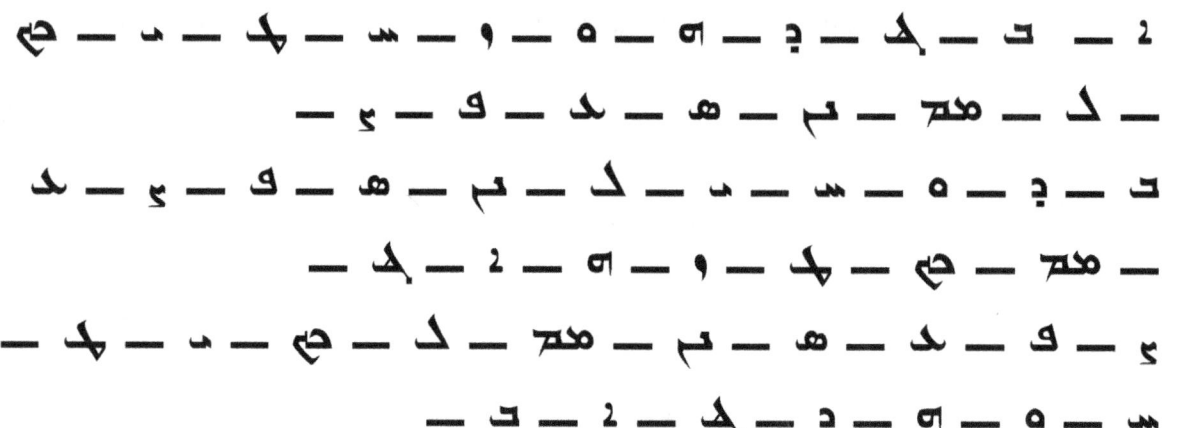

3- Write the following numbers in Aramaic.

10 _____	18 _____	20 _____	29 _____	30 _____	33 _____
40 _____	47 _____	50 _____	52 _____	60 _____	63 _____
70 _____	74 _____	80 _____	85 _____	90 _____	95 _____

4- Practice reading: The letters with their vowels.

ܗܒ݂ ܠܒ݂ ܩܒ݂ ܪܒ݂

5- Translate and transliterate the following words.

ܩܵܒ݂ܵܐ

ܡܸܠܩܵܢܵܐ

ܫܒ݂ܵܩܵܐ

ܟܘܼܒ݂ܵܐ

ܢܘܼܒ݂ܵܐ

ܥܸܠܒ݂ܵܐ

ܣܝܼܒ݂ܵܐ

ܒ݂ܠܝܼܬܵܐ

ܒ݂ܢܵܐ

ܠܒ݂ܢܵܐ

ܢܠܒ݂ܵܐ

ܗܒ݂ܵܐ

ܗܘܒ݂ܢܵܐ

ܟܸܢܒ݂ܵܐ

47

UNIT SIX

The Sixth Group of Letters:
Q   R   SH   T   (Qarshut)

THE LETTER QOP ܩܘܦ ܩ - Q

Qop has no precise equivalent English letter. It is transliterated by using the letter Q. Qop has a palatal sound. The numerical value of Qop is 100. Thus, ܩܐ is 101, ܩܝܒ is 112 and ܩܢܗ is 155. Beginning with Qop ܩ each succeeding letter is by hundreds until Taw - 400. The higher figure is always first (on the right side) then it is followed by tens and then by single figures. Thus, when 123 is written – Qop first, followed by Kap, then gamal = ܩܟܓ The letter Qop is written in the following manner: ܩ

- A- Begin at the right side of the page. Make a downward vertical stroke*. (see *Note: beth, p. 4).

- B- Make a medium horizontal line from the top of the vertical stroke.

- C- Beginning from the base of the vertical line make a horizontal line almost the length of the top horizontal line then slightly curve the stroke into a vertical line touching the top horizontal line.

- D- Complete the letter by making a very short horizontal line at the left corner of the letter.

- E- Write the letter Qop ܩ, ten times.

F- Write the following words five times.

58. Wood – Qaisa – ܩܝܣܐ _____ _____ _____ _____ _____

59. Mosquito – Baqa – ܒܩܐ _____ _____ _____ _____ _____

60. Cat – Qita – ܩܛܐ _____ _____ _____ _____ _____

61. Blossom – Piqha – ܦܩܚܐ _____ _____ _____ _____ _____

62. Monkey – Qopa – ܩܘܦܐ _____ _____ _____ _____ _____

63. Nose – Poqa – ܦܘܩܐ _____ _____ _____ _____ _____

Qop connects to any letter which follows it. When it is a medial letter, it is joined on both sides. (See **NOTE, p. 4).

THE LETTER RESH ܪܝܫ ܪ - R

Resh is equivalent to the English letter R. It has a lingual sound. The numerical value of Resh is 200. Thus, ܪܒ is 202, ܪܟܒ is 222 and ܪܨܒ is 292. (See the letter Qop, p. 48, the higher numbers preceding the lesser figures). The letter Resh is written in the following manner: ܪ

A- Begin at the right side of the page. Make a horizontal line from right to left.

_____

B- Make a curved line moving from right to left over the short horizontal line.

_____

C- Make a short horizontal line above the letter.

_____

D- Write the letter Resh ܪ, R, ten times.

_____ _____ _____ _____ _____ _____ ܕ.

_____ _____ _____ _____ _____

E- Write the following words five times:

64. Bone - Garma - ܓܲܪܡܵܐ _____ _____ _____ _____

65. Moon – Sahra - ܣܲܗܪܵܐ _____ _____ _____ _____

66. Great - Raba - ܪܲܒܵܐ _____ _____ _____ _____

67. Spirit, Wind - Ruha - ܪܘܼܚܵܐ _____ _____ _____ _____

68. Friend - Rahma - ܪܲܚܡܵܐ _____ _____ _____ _____

69. High - Rama - ܪܵܡܵܐ _____ _____ _____ _____

70. Foot - Righla - ܪܸܓ݂ܠܵܐ _____ _____ _____ _____

The letter Resh in Estrangela is shaped differently and is written in the following manner: ܪ

A- Begin at the right side of the page. Make a short vertical line in a downwards stroke.

_____ ܐ

B- Make a short horizontal line from right to left joined at the top of the vertical line.

_____ ܂

C- Place a dot above the horizontal line.

_____ ܪ

D- Write the letter Resh ܪ , R, ten times.

_____ _____ _____ _____ _____ ܪ

_____ _____ _____ _____ _____

Resh never connects to any letter which follows it. (See Ch. 2, Rule 2). When it is a medial letter, it is joined on the right side only.

THE LETTER SHEEN ܫܝܢ ܫ - SH

Sheen is equivalent to the English letters SH. It has a dental sound (Sibilant). The numerical value of Sheen is 300. Thus, ܫܓ is 303, ܫܛ is 309 and ܫܠܓ is 333. (See the letter Qop, p. 48, the higher numbers preceding the lesser figures). The letter Sheen is written in the following manner: ܫ

A- Begin at the right side of the page. Make a very short horizontal line with an upward vertical stroke.

B- Make a short horizontal line over the top of the vertical line from right to left.

C- Retrace the vertical stroke downwards and make a short horizontal line to the left.

D- Write the letter Sheen ܫ , Sh, ten times.

E- Write the following words five times.

71. Head – Resha - ܪܹܫܵܐ _____ _____ _____ _____

72. Deacon – Shamasha - ܫܲܡܵܫܵܐ _____ _____ _____ _____

73. Priest, Old Man - Qashisha ܩܲܫܝܼܫܵܐ _____ _____ _____ _____

51

74. Sun – Shemsha - ܫܸܡܫܵܐ _____ _____ _____ _____
_____

75. Man, Human being – Barnasha - ܒܲܪܢܵܫܵܐ _____ _____ _____
_____ _____

76. Apostle – Shleeha - ܫܠܝܼܚܵܐ _____ _____ _____ _____
_____

77. Peace – Shlama - ܫܠܵܡܵܐ _____ _____ _____ _____
_____

78. Evil – Beesha - ܒܝܼܫܵܐ _____ _____ _____ _____
_____

79. Evening – Ramsha - ܪܲܡܫܵܐ _____ _____ _____ _____
_____

80. Jesus – Eshoa - ܝܼܫܘܿܥ _____ _____ _____ _____
_____

Sheen connects to any letter which follows it. When it is medial letter, it is joined on both sides. (See **NOTE, p. 4).

THE LETTER TAW ܬܘ̈ ܬ - T

Taw is equivalent to the English letter T. It has a lingual sound. When a dot is placed beneath the Taw ܬ it becomes soft <u>Th</u> as in <u>th</u>ird. The numerical value of Taw is 400. Thus, ܬܕ is 404, ܬܡܕ is 444 and ܬܡܚ is 448. (See the letter Qop, p. 48, the higher number preceding the lesser figures). The letter Taw is written in the following manner: ܬ

A- Begin at the right side of the page. Make a long slanted downward stroke* to the right. (See *Note: Beth, p. 3).

B- Beginning at the top of the slanted line make a downward slanted stroke to the left forming a tent.

C- Make a short loop from the left slanted line to the right.

D- Write the letter Taw ܬ , ten times.

_____ _____ _____ _____ . ܬ

_____ _____ _____ _____ _____

E- Write the following words five times.

81. Snow – Talga - ܬܲܠܓܵܐ _____ _____ _____ _____

_____

82. Bull – Taura - ܬܵܘܪܵܐ _____ _____ _____ _____

_____

83. Linen, Cloth – Kitana - ܟܹܬܵܢܵܐ _____ _____ _____ _____

_____

84. Student, Disciple – Talmeedha - ܬܲܠܡܝܼܕܵܐ _____ _____ _____

_____ _____

85. Prayer – Slotha - ܨܠܘܿܬܵܐ _____ _____ _____ _____

_____

86. Glory – Tishbohta - ܬܸܫܒܘܿܚܬܵܐ _____ _____ _____ _____

_____

87. Service – Tishmishta - ܬܸܫܡܸܫܬܵܐ _____ _____ _____ _____

_____ _____

NOTE: There are some orthographies who give Taw another shape and it is in frequent use today. The writers of Aramaic are free to use whichever form of Taw they choose.

    A- Begin at the right side of the page. Make a short vertical line.

    B- Join a loop to the vertical stroke.

    C- Make a short slanted upward line to the left of the loop.

    D- Write Taw in this form ten times.

_____ _____ _____ _____ _____
_____ _____ _____ _____ _____

The letter Taw in Estrangela is shaped differently and is written in the following manner:

    A- Begin at the right side of the page. Make a short downward vertical stroke*. (See *Note: Beth, p. 3).

    B- Make a medium horizontal line beginning at the top of the first line.

    C- Beginning on the left of the horizontal line make a loop to the right terminating in a vertical stroke.

    D- Write the letter Taw ten times.

_____ _____ _____ _____ _____
_____ _____ _____ _____ _____

    Taw never connects to any letter which follows it. (See Ch. 2, rule 2). When it is a medial letter, it is joined on the right side only.

REVIEW

1- The Aramaic letters ܒ - ܬ written in relation to each other.

ܒܓܕܗܘܙܚܛܝܟܠܡܢܣܥܦܨܩܪܫܬ

2- Write the letters smikath ܣ through Taw ܬ.

_____ _____ _____ _____ _____ _____

3- Write the following numbers in Aramaic.

100 ____	110 ____	120 ____	130 ____	140 ____
150 ____	160 ____	170 ____	180 ____	190 ____
200 ____	201 ____	212 ____	223 ____	234 ____
245 ____	256 ____	278 ____	289 ____	299 ____
300 ____	350 ____	388 ____	400 ____	499 ____ .

4- Identify the following letters by name and transliterate in the Roman (English) alphabet.

ܒ _ ܓ _ ܕ _ ܗ _ ܘ _ ܙ _ ܚ _ ܛ _ ܝ _ ܟ _ ܠ _

ܡ _ ܢ _ ܣ _ ܥ _ ܦ _ ܨ _ ܩ _ ܪ _ ܫ _ ܬ _ ܒ _

ܓ _ ܗ _ ܘ _ ܚ _ ܝ _ ܠ _ ܢ _ ܥ _ ܨ _ ܪ _ ܬ _ ܕ _

ܛ _ ܟ _ ܡ _ ܣ _ ܦ _ ܩ _ ܫ _ ܠ _ ܘ _ ܒ _ ܬ _

ܕ _ ܛ _ ܥ _ ܦ _ ܠ _ ܗ _ ܟ _ ܡ _ ܣ _ ܩ _ ܪ _

ܫ _ ܚ _ ܘ _ ܗ _ ܕ _ ܓ _ ܒ _ ܙ _ .

5- Practice reading: The letters with their vowels.

$$
\begin{array}{cccc}
\text{ܒܹ} & \text{ܒܹ} & \text{ܕܹ} & \text{ܡܹ} \\
\text{ܗܹ} & \text{ܒܹ} & \text{ܕܹ} & \text{ܡܹ} \\
\text{ܗܿ} & \text{ܫܿ} & \text{ܕܿ} & \text{ܣܿ} \\
\text{ܗܼ} & \text{ܫܼ} & \text{ܕܼ} & \text{ܣܼ} \\
\text{ܗܝ} & \text{ܫܝ} & \text{ܕܝ} & \text{ܡܝ}
\end{array}
$$

6- Translate and transliterate the following vocabulary.

ܥܲܡܵܐ

ܒܹܐܪܵܐ

ܒܝܼܟ݂ܵܐ

ܕܲܡܵܐ

ܕܝܼܣܵܐ

ܕܘܼܢܹܐ

ܕܲܢܹܐ

ܗܲܘܕܵܐ

ܟܲܕܡܵܐ

ܟܲܘܬ݂ܵܐ

ܣܵܘܩܵܐ

ܩܡܼܢܵܐ

_____ _____

_____ _____

_____ _____

_____ _____

_____ _____

_____ _____

_____ _____

_____ _____

_____ _____

_____ _____

_____ _____

ܡܝܬܪ

ܬܢܝ

ܢܩܝܦ

ܡܥܬܦܣܢܐ

ܡܥܩܒܢܐ

ܥܠܩܘܢܐ

ܡܠܥܒܢܐ

ܚܕܬܐ

ܗܘܕܐ

ܡܠܟܐ

ܢܥܡܕ

ܕܝܠܢ

ܛܝܢܐ

ܥܠܩܦܐ

ܥܠܝܢܐ

ܓܕܢܦܐ

ܝܡܢܐ

ܢܥܝܢܐ

THE ARAMAIC ALPHABET

ENGLISH	ESTRANGELA	NUMBER	ALPHABET	NAME
A	ܐ	1	ܐ	ܐܵܠܲܦ
B – W		2	ܒ	ܒܹܝܬ
G – GH		3	ܓ ܓ	ܓܵܡܲܠ
D – DH	ܕ	4	ܕ - ܕ	ܕܵܠܲܕ
H	ܗ	5	ܗ	ܗܹܐ
W		6	ܘ	ܘܵܘ
Z		7	ܙ	ܙܲܝܢ
H		8	ܚ	ܚܹܝܬ
T		9	ܛ	ܛܹܝܬ
Y		10	ܝ	ܝܘܿܕ
K – KH		20	ܟ - ܟ	ܟܵܦ
FINAL K			ܟ - ܟ	ܟܵܦ
L		30	ܠ	ܠܵܡܲܕ
M	ܡ	40	ܡ	ܡܹܝܡ
FINAL M				ܡܡ

N		50	ܢ	ܢܘܿ
FINAL N			ܢ - ܢ	ܢ
S		60	ܣ	ܣܡܟ݂
A		70	ܥ	ܥܹܐ
P – W		80	ܦ - ܦ	ܦܹܐ
S		90	ܨ	ܨܵܕܹܐ
Q		100	ܩ	ܩܘܿܦ
R	ܪ	200	ܪ	ܪܹܫ
SH		300	ܫ	ܫܝܼܢ
T – TH	ܬ	400	ܐ - ܬ	ܬܵܘ

GRAND REVIEW

1- Practice reading the letters with their vowels.

ܒܼ ܒܼ ܒ݂ ܒ݁ ܒ݂ ܒܼ ܒܼ ܒ݂ ܒܼ ܒܼ ܒܼ ܒܼ ܒܼ ܒܼ ܒܼ ܒܼ ܒܼ

ܒܼ ܒܼ ܒܼ ܒܼ ܒܼ ܒܼ ܒܼ ܒܼ ܒܼ ܒܼ ܒܼ ܒܼ ܒܼ ܒܼ

ܠܼ ܠܼ ܠܼ ܠܼ ܠܼ ܠܼ ܠܼ ܠܼ ܠܼ ܠܼ ܠܼ ܠܼ ܠܼ ܠܼ ܠܼ ܠܼ

2- Write the Aramaic alphabet. (Begin at the right side of the page).

_____ _____ _____ _____ _____ _____ _____

_____ _____ _____ _____ _____ _____ _____

_____ _____ _____ _____ _____ _____ _____

3- Name and write the seven vowels and gives an example for each vowel.
1) _____ _____ _____
2) _____ _____ _____
3) _____ _____ _____
4) _____ _____ _____
5) _____ _____ _____
6) _____ _____ _____
7) _____ _____ _____

4- Write the four Bdhol letters. (Begins at the right side of the page).

_____ _____ _____ _____

5- Write the three weak letters.

_____ _____ _____

6- Write the conjunction - and - _____

7- Write the six letters which become soft.

_____ _____ _____ _____ _____ _____

8- Write the eight letters that never connect to any letters which follow them.

9- Write the six Estrangela letters which differ from Classical Aramaic.

10- Write the letters which change shape when final. (Distinguish the letters which are joined and not joined).
1) _____   _____
2) _____   _____
3) _____   _____

GRAND VOCABULARY REVIEW

Transliterate and translate into English the following words.

ܟܰܕ

ܟܶܢܶܐ

ܠܰܚܡܳܐ

ܕܶܢܶܐ

ܚܓ݂ܺܕ݂ܺܕ݂

ܬܳܗ̈ܳܐ

ܠܶܒܶܐ

ܟܶܢܳܐ

ܠܰܘܢܰܐ

ܠܳܗ̈ܳܐ

ܒܘ̈ܒܶܐ

ܠܳܘܕ̈ܶܐ

ܦܰܠܦܶܐ

61

ܢܘܢܐ
ܩܘܦܐ
ܡܠܐܟܐ
ܫܡܫܐ
ܩܛܐ
ܒܝܬܟܬܒܐ
ܠܚܡܐ
ܒܪܬܐ
ܨܦܪܐ
ܚܠܒܐ
ܣܝܦܐ
ܛܝܣܐ
ܘܪܕܐ
ܓܢܒܪܐ
ܒܪܐ
ܣܘܣܐ
ܡܝܐ
ܬܐܢܐ
ܩܡܚܐ
ܡܠܟܐ
ܝܡܐ
ܚܘܫܒܢܐ

ܐܒܝܬܐ
ܣܝܟܬܐ
ܩܘܦܐ
ܟܕܒܐ
ܗܓܕܐ
ܕܒܐ
ܙܒܕܐ
ܚܕܐ
ܛܘܒܐ
ܕܘܒܐ
ܢܣܩܐ
ܝܕܐ
ܟܘܟܒܐ
ܠܒܟܐ
ܡܘܡܐ
ܕܘܦ
ܥܝܢ
ܕܥܐ
ܨܘܦܐ
ܠܐ
ܝܬܐ
ܡܥܠܐ

ܝܡܡܐ
ܐܬܐ
ܫܠܡܐ
ܒܪܬܐ
ܥܠܝܡܐ
ܡܠܟܐ
ܫܒܝܛܐ
ܥܠܡܐ
ܚܒܪܐ
ܫܠܡܐ
ܝܘܡܐ
ܒܥܠܕ
ܒܝܬܐ
ܕܡܥܐ
ܡܠܟܐ
ܗܘܕܐ
ܓܒܪܐ
ܫܢܬܐ
ܝܕܐ
ܒܠܬܐ
ܢܘܢ
ܩܝܣܐ

ܟܬܒܐ _____   _____
ܘܬܠܡܝܕܐ _____   _____
ܘܩܘܕܫܐ _____   _____
ܘܥܡܕܐ _____   _____

READING
THE GOSPEL OF MATTHEW
CHAPTER ONE

ܐ . ܟܬܒܐ ܕܝܠܝܕܘܬܗ ܕܝܫܘܥ ܡܫܝܚܐ ܒܪܗ ܕܕܘܝܕ ܒܪܗ ܕܐܒܪܗܡ .

ܒ . ܐܒܪܗܡ ܐܘܠܕ ܠܐܝܣܚܩ . ܐܝܣܚܩ ܐܘܠܕ ܠܝܥܩܘܒ . ܝܥܩܘܒ ܐܘܠܕ ܠܝܗܘܕܐ ܘܠܐܚܘܗܝ .

ܓ . ܝܗܘܕܐ ܐܘܠܕ ܠܦܪܨ ܘܠܙܪܚ ܡܢ ܬܡܪ . ܦܪܨ ܐܘܠܕ ܠܚܨܪܘܢ . ܚܨܪܘܢ ܐܘܠܕ ܠܐܪܡ .

ܕ . ܐܪܡ ܐܘܠܕ ܠܥܡܝܢܕܒ . ܥܡܝܢܕܒ ܐܘܠܕ ܠܢܚܫܘܢ . ܢܚܫܘܢ ܐܘܠܕ ܠܣܠܡܘܢ .

UNIT SEVEN

The Origin of the Alphabet

The Sumerians and Egyptians began their language with pictures (symbols). Later on these symbols were developed into an alphabet. The ancient Assyrians shaped their alphabet from objects and things. The following is a very short summation showing how the Estrangela letters were derived.

1- ܐ Alap, the first letter of the Aramaic alphabet was shaped like an ox head, one of the gods of Mesopotamia.

2- ܒ Beth was shaped like an ancient house. (Bayta - ܒܲܝܬܵܐ , house).

3- ܓ Gamal resembled a Camel's saddle. (Gamla - ܓܲܡܠܵܐ , Camel and in English a camel's hump).

4- ܕ Dalath resembled a field at the mouth of a river, also delta or triangle.

5- ܗ Heh resembled a trap, or a pit. (Hauta - ܚܵܘܬܵܐ , a ditch)

6- ܘ Waw resembled the shape of a flower which was opening. (Warda - ܘܲܪܕܵܐ - Flower)

7- ܙ Zain resembled the head of a weapon – an arrow or a spear. (Zayna - ܙܲܝܢܵܐ - Weapon)

8- ܚ Heth resembled a snake in motion. (Hiwya - ܚܘܝܵܐ - Snake)

9- ܛ Teth resembled a bird (Tayra - ܛܲܝܪܵܐ - Bird)

10- ܝ Yodh resembled a half – opened palm of the hand as one who is begging. (Eedha - ܐܝܼܕܵܐ - Hand)

11- ܟ Kap resembled a fist - a closed hand.

12- ܠ Lamadh resembled a jaw bone.

13- ܡ Meem resembled the shape of a pond with water in it. (Maya - ܡܲܝܵܐ - Water).

14- ܢ Noon resembled an axe (Narga - ܢܲܪܓܵܐ - Axe)

15- ܣ Simkath resembled the moon with a face. The moon was the goddess of all Mesopotamia. (Sahra - ܣܲܗܪܵܐ - moon).

16- ܥ Ae resembled a side view of an open eye, especially a human eye. (Ayna - ܥܲܝܢܵܐ - eye).

17- ܦ Peth resembled the shape of a mouth. (Pooma - ܦܘܿܡܵܐ - mouth; Poqa - ܦܘܿܩܵܐ - nose).

18- ܨ Sadhe resembled a statue. (Salma - ܨܲܠܡܵܐ - idol/status/face).

19- ܩ Qop resembled an ancient basket made of reeds. (Qupa – ܩܘܿܦܵܐ - basket).

20- ܪ Resh resembled the human head with a small curl of hair. (Resha - - Head).

21- ܫ Sheen resembled an ancient eastern lamp. (Shragha – ܫܪܵܓܵܐ - lamp).

22- ܬ Taw resembled a jar. (Talma - ܬܲܠܡܵܐ - jar).

ARAMAIC ALPHABETS

Estrangela	Classical	Western or Chaldean (also used in Hebrew)
ܐ	ܐ	א
ܒ	ܒ	ב
ܓ	ܓ	ג
ܕ	ܕ	ד
ܗ	ܗ	ה
ܘ	ܘ	ו
ܙ	ܙ	ז
ܚ	ܚ	ח
ܛ	ܛ	ט
ܝ	ܝ	י
ܟ	ܟ	כ ך
ܠ	ܠ	ל
ܡ	ܡ	מ ם

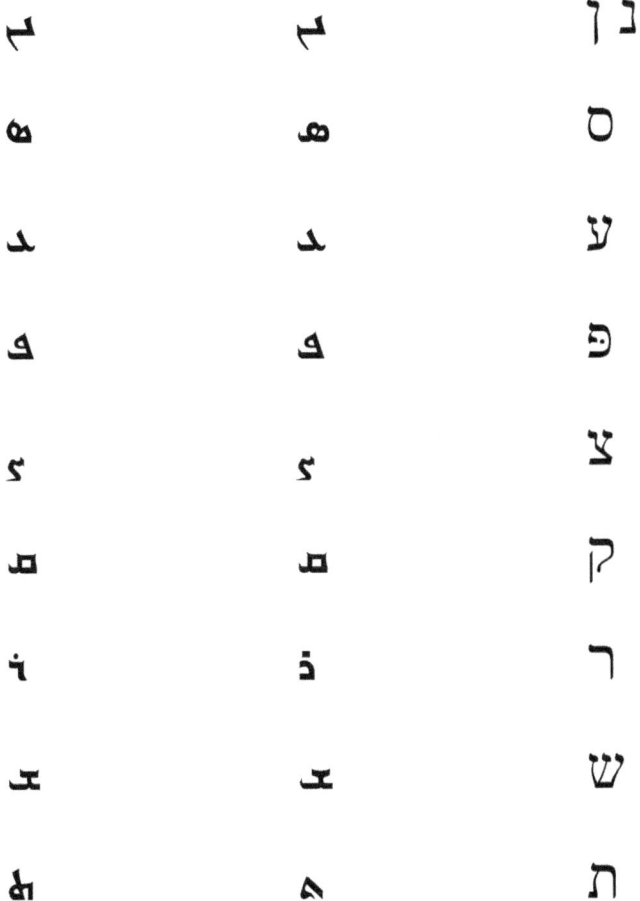

The alphabet used in writing all traditional text of the Hebrew Bible is more precisely Aramaic than Hebrew. The Aramaic secular letters known as Western or Chaldean letters (also called "square letters" by the Europeans) were employed in Hebrew papyri and parchments in the second and first centuries B.C. and are attested as the normal alphabet for writing Hebrew from that time to our present day. According to Rabbinic sources, Ezra, the great Jewish leader, priest, scribe, wise student and teacher of the Torah had chosen the secular Aramaic alphabet for the writing of the Torah instead of the ancient Hebrew letters. Beginning with the Babylonian (Chaldean) captivity Aramaic as the popular language had been slowly and gradually replacing Hebrew; therefore the change in the shape of the letters was meant to facilitate the study of the Torah by the people.

CHAPTER TWO

GENERAL BASIC RULES

GENERAL BASIC RULES

1- The letters of the Aramaic alphabet and their vocal placement:

A- GUTTURALS ܓܲܓܪܵܢܹ̈ܐ are formed in the throat back of the tongue and the soft palate. The gutturals are: ܥ. ܚ. ܗ. ܐ. Some grammarians add the letter resh.

B- LINGUALS are formed by the tip of the tongue. The linguals are:

ܕ. ܛ. ܠ. ܢ. ܬ. ܬ.

C- PALATALS ܚܸܟܵܢܹ̈ܐ are made with the front or middle of the tongue near or touching the roof of the mouth. The palatals are: ܓ. ܝ. ܟ. ܩ.

D- DENTALS ܫܸܢܵܢܹ̈ܐ are formed with the teeth, a sibilant. The dentals are:

ܙ. ܣ. ܨ. ܫ.

E- LABIALS ܣܸܦܘܵܢܹ̈ܐ a sound pronounced with the lips closed, nearly closed, or rounded. The Labials are: ܒ. ܘ. ܡ. ܦ.

2- The Eight Letters occurring in a word which are not joined to their following letters.

ܐ. ܕ. ܗ. ܘ. ܙ. ܥ. ܨ. ܬ.

When one of these letters is a medial letter and it is not preceded by another one of the unjoined letters, then the letter is connected on right side only.

3- The Three Weak Letters ܐ. ܘ. ܝ. were used as vowels before the introduction of the vowel (points) signs. Alap denoted A, long A, and E. Waw ܘ - denoted the OO, U and O. Yodh ܝ - denoted I. They are called weak letters because they change their sound. Strong letters do not change.

4- The Four B D O L letters: Maplatha ܡܲܦܠܲܬܼܵܐ B D O L; ܒ ܕ ܘ ܠ - (Bdhol).

NOTE: The Bdhol letters are prefixed to a noun, i.e, they precede the noun.

Examples

The king	ܡܠܟܐ
In, with, by, through the king	ܒ - ܒܡܠܟܐ
Of, from, the king	ܕ - ܕܡܠܟܐ
And the king	ܘ - ܘܡܠܟܐ
To, for the king	ܠ - ܠܡܠܟܐ

5- The Six Estrangela letters which differ in shape from Classical Aramaic.

1- ܐ A - Alap

2- ܕ D - Dalath

3- ܗ H - Heh

4- ܡ M - Meem

5- ܪ R - Resh

6- ܬ T - Taw

REMINDER: Meem only changes shapes as an initial or medial letter in Estrangela. (See Ch. 1, P. 32). The vowel signs or pointing system were not and are not used with Estrangela letters, except the plural sign, siyame, ܗܢܡܐ

The Seven Vowels ܙܘܥܐ

ܐ̇	Zqapa	ܘܩܦܐ
ܐ̣	Pthaha	ܦܬܚܐ
ܐ̤	Zlama Psheeqa	ܙܠܡܐ ܦܫܝܩܐ

74

	Zlama Qashya	ܘܲܠܓܲܕ݂ ܡܥܲܢܹܐ
	Rwaha	ܕܿܘܵܫܹܐ
	Rwasa	ܕܿܢܹܐ
	Hwasa	ܣܬܼܢܹܐ

7- Doubling or duplicating of letters in nouns and verbs (only in pronunciation, not writing)

A- A vocalized letter ܬ which follows a letter with a Pthaha ○ or Zlama Psheeqa ܒ is doubled in pronunciation only.

NOUNS

Cook	ܛܲܒ݂ܵܚܵܐ	Pronounced – Tabbaha
Bold	ܡܲܪܵܚܵܐ	Pronounced – Marraha
Bear	ܕܸܒܵܐ	Pronounced – Dibba
Heart	ܠܸܒܵܐ	Pronounced – Libba

Exceptions

God	ܐܲܠܵܗܵܐ	Pronounced – alaha
Father	ܐܲܒܵܐ	Pronounced – awa

Verbs

To make joyful	ܗܲܕܹܐ	Pronounced – Hadde
To destroy	ܗܲܒܸܠ	Pronounced – Habbel

75

NOTE: If a vocalized letter which follows the letter with a Pthaha ◌ is Aeh ܚ or Resh ܪ, there is no doubling and the Pthaha vocalizing the first letter is pronounced as a Zqapa ◌

Examples

To reconcile   ܪܵܥܹܐ   Pronounced – Raaee

To bless   ܒܵܪܹܟ݂   Pronounced – Barekh

To begin   ܫܵܪܹܐ   Pronounced – Sharee

B- Both Pthaha and Zlama psheeqa ◌ and ◌ are considered short vowels and usually when a vocalized letter follows them, it doubles in sound and never in writing. However there are a few words which double in sound but do not follow a Pthaha or Zlama psheeqa.

Love   ܚܘܼܒܵܐ   Pronounced – Hubba

Chest, Breast   ܥܘܼܒܵܐ   Pronounced – Aubba

8- Syame ܣܝܵܡܹ̈ܐ the Plural Points.

Two big points horizontally marked above a letter in a word are plural in nouns, collective nouns, and adjective and in certain forms of the verbs.

NOTE: The two large points are usually placed over the middle letters, which do not rise above the line, or over a non- vocalized letter. However, when the letter resh ܪ is in the word, the short horizontal line over the resh will not appear but the plural points are used instead ܪ̈ When resh has a Zqapa and a syame only one point is added over the left syame to form the Zqapa - ܪ̈ ܥܒ݂ܝܼܕܹ̈ܐ if there is more than one resh in a word, the points will be placed on the final

76

resh - ܕܘܿܕܹܪ When every letter in a word is vocalized and there is no resh, the syame is placed between letters - ܡܵܝ̈ܐ

Nouns

Teacher   ܡܲܠܦܵܢܵܐ   - Malpana

Teachers   ܡܲܠܦܵܢܹ̈ܐ   - Malpane

Man   ܓܲܒ݂ܪܵܐ   - Gawra

Men   ܓܲܒ݂ܪܹ̈ܐ   - Gawre

Collective Noun

Water   ܡܲܝ̈ܐ   Maya

Adjective Noun

Good   ܛܵܒܹ̈ܐ   ܛܵܒ݂ܵܐ

Bad   ܒܝܼܫܹ̈ܐ   ܒܝܼܫܵܐ

Verbs

They wrote   ܟܬ݂ܝܼܒ̈ܝ   - Feminine Plural

They write   ܟܵܬ̈ܒܵܢ   - Feminine Plural

You write   ܟܵܬ̈ܒܝܼܬܹܝܢ   - Feminine Plural

9- Nugze Raurwe ܢܘܼܩܙܹܐ ܪܲܘܪ̈ܒܹܐ the Points of Distinction.

A- Points of distinction are big points used either as one point alone or as two points (pair) above or beneath a word to indicate proper reading and meaning.

In Verbs

He killed   ܩܛܲܠ   or He saved   ܦܪܲܩ

The large point under the ܒ indicate past tense.

He writes   ܟܵܬܹܒ

He kills   ܩܵܛܹܠ

The large point over the middle letter indicates present tense.

He killed her   ܩܛܲܠܵܗ̇

The large point is placed above the heh ܗ̇ and indicates the feminine pronoun "her". The pronoun is suffixed to the verb.

B- The two large points underneath Heh ܗ̤ indicate past tense.

He was   ܗ̤ܘܵܐ

10- Mhagyana   ܡܗܲܓܝܵܢܵܐ   The vocalizer.

A vocalizer appears by placing a short horizontal line under one of the following letters occurring in a word when they follow another non-vocalized letter.

ܐ ܗ ܘ ܚ ܠ ܡ ܢ ܥ ܪ   (simply phrased: Amlay nuhra   ܥܡܠܲܝ ܢܘܼܗܪܵܐ)

This line means that a non-vocalized letter which precedes the underscored letter receives the vowel sound of Zlama psheeqa   ܠܝܼܛܵܐ   accursed and   ܡܲܢܗܲܪ   illuminate. Thus, the sound of the vowel joins both non-vocalized letters and creates a closed syllable as in wisdom

ܚܸܟܡܬܵܐ   and bed   ܡܕܲܡܟ݂ܵܐ .

11- Marhtana   ܡܲܪܗܛܵܢܵܐ   the Hastener. Speedy

When two non-vocalized letters occur in a word and the second is not one of the nine (ܥܡܠܲܝ ܢܘܼܗܪܵܐ), a hastener is placed above the first non-vocalized letter indicated by a slanted line. Example: drink Mashtya   ܡܲܫܬܝܵܐ . It is similar to making the word into two syllables. The first non-vocalized letter ends the first syllable ܡܫ (mash) and the second non-vocalized letter begins the second syllable ܬܝܐ (tya).

12- Mwatlana ܡܬܚܠܢܐ the Suppressor.

The suppressor is indicated by a slanted line above certain letters. The line indicates that the letter becomes silent. The letters are: ܕ ܛ ܚ ܟ ܠ ܢ ܥ ܬ

Examples: ܢܫܐ Nasha - man, ܐܬ At – you, ܐܪܙܐ Raza - mystery, secret.

13- Occulted Letters. (ܣܘܩܢܐ) Hidden

A- In addition to the above eight letters there are four more letters which become silent but do not carry the sign of the mwatlana. They are: ܒ ܘ ܝ ܬ

Examples -

Church ܒ - ܒܝܕܬܐ   They did ܘ - ܥܒܕܘ

ܝ - ܡܠܟܝ My king   ܬ - ܡܬܬܢܝܚ passive voice of the verb - to rest.

B- Letters which are pronounced but are not written: In contrast to point A. there are some words which have a hidden, unwritten letter, or sound.

Examples: ܟܠ Kap and lamadh are the only letters written in the word but is pronounced Kol, which means All.

ܡܛܠ Meem, teth and lamadh are the only letters written in the word but it is pronounced Mittol. In both words "Kol and Mittol" there is a hidden rwaha. ܘ - ܩܘܫܬܐ

ܫܬܐ Sheen, taw and alap are the only letters written in the word with a zqapa above the taw but is is pronounced Isht. Note: The letter alap is hidden and it carries zlama psheeqa – (ܐܫܬܐ).

ܫܬܐ Means six. [See p. 86].

14- Accent: In Aramaic there are no written rules for accent (stress). The following is only a general idea.

A- When a word ends in consonant the stress falls on the last syllable.

Examples:

ܡܰܪܝܰܡ Maryam Mary,   ܚܰܡܝܫ Hamish five.

ܬܰܪܓܝܡ Targim to interpret.

B- When a word ends in a vowel, the accent or stress falls on the next to the last syllable.
   Example: ܡܰܠܟܳܐ Malka - King.

15- Syllables:

A- A syllable is formed by a vocalized letter. There are two kinds of syllables, closed and open.

B- A closed syllable ends in one or more non-vocalized consonants as in Marqos (Markos) - ܡܰܪܩܳܘܣ Mark and Lait - ܠܰܝܬ (there is or are none).

C- An open syllable ends in a vowel which may be followed by another vocalized letter, or not, as in Mana - ܡܳܢܳܐ what, and Tawatha - ܛܳܒ̈ܬܳܐ good things.

D- Some words have closed and open syllable as in Qarqaptha - ܩܰܪܩܰܦܬܳܐ skull.

16- Qushaya and Rukakha: Hard and Soft Letters.

There are six letters may be pronounced in two ways, either as hard (original sound) or soft, which changes the original to a sound.

Qushaya, ܩܘܫܳܝܳܐ, means hard, Rukakha, ܪܘܟܳܟܳܐ, means soft (sound). The six letters are B G D K P T and are called ܒܓܕܟܦܬ Bgadhikpath letters. These letters change to "sounds"

B changes to W	ܒ ܒ	ܘܰܐ	wha
G changes to Gh	ܓ ܓ	ܓܰܐ	gha
D changes to Dh	ܕ ܕ	ܕܰܐ	dha
K change to Kh	ܟ ܟ	ܟܰܐ	kha

P changes to W	ܦ ܝ	ܦ݁	wha
T changes to Th	ܬ ܚ	ܬ݁	tha

NOTE: As the Aramaic language developed, in needed six additional letters to adapt itself to neighboring languages. When the six letters were added, for some unknown reason, two of the six letters were not new. ܒ and ܦ were aspirated and became the letter W. However, the Aramaic alphabet already contained the letter W ܘ , waw.

The six letters become hard or soft according to the following rules:

QUSHAYA ܩܘܫܝܐ In hardening the letters B G D K P T only five of them follow the rules A through F. Peh is the exception. Peh is always hard when it occurs in a word unless it is written as ܦ . There are about 22 Aramaic words in which peh becomes a soft and changes to a W. Examples: Soul - ܢܦܫܐ

A- When any of the five letters BGDKT begin a word, they are hard as in the following;

Son	ܒܪܐ	Bra
Man	ܓܒܪܐ	Gawra
Judgment	ܕܝܢܐ	Deena
Bride	ܟܠܬܐ	Kaltha
Student	ܬܠܡܝܕܐ	Talmeedha

B- When any of the five are vocalized and are preceded by a letter with a pthaha ◌ܲ or zlama psheeqa ◌ܸ they remain hard.

Examples
Pthaha

Bell	ܙܓܳܐ	- Zaga
Great	ܪܰܒܳܐ	- Raba

Zlama Psheeqa

Track	ܣܺܟܳܐ	- Sika

Exceptions

Eat	ܐܺܟܰܠ	- Ikhal
Lost	ܐܺܘܰܕ݂	- Iwadh

C- When any of the five letters are vocalized and are preceded by a Rwaha ܘ̇ or Rwasa ܘ̣ which are vocalizing the initial letter of a word, the letters become hard. (But when any of the five letters are non-vocalized then they become soft. Example: ܩܘܕܫܐ - Qoodhsha.

Examples

Den – well	ܓܘܒܳܐ	- Gooba
Wall	ܓܘܕܳܐ	- Guda
Foolish	ܒܘܕܳܐ	- Boda
Love	ܚܘܒܳܐ	- Hooba
Chest - Womb	ܥܘܒܳܐ	- Auba

D- When any of the five letters are preceded by a non-vocalized medial letter in the word it remains hard.

Examples

Martyr	ܣܗܕܐ	- Sahda
Skin	ܡܫܟܐ	- Mishka

Exception to the rule: if the non-vocalized letter which precedes one of the five is an alap ܐ or a yodh ܝ, it will not become hard.

Examples

Suffering	ܟܐܒܐ	- Kewa
Feast	ܥܐܕܐ	- Aedha
House of, family	ܒܝܬ	- Beth

E- When any of the five letters terminate a word and are preceded by a non-vocalized letter. They remain hard.

There is none	ܠܝܬ	- Lait
You created	ܒܪܝܬ	- Brayt

Exception

House of, family	ܒܝܬ	- Beth

F- When any of the five letters occur as a third letter in a word and the first letter is with a Pthaha, it becomes hard.

Spear, sword	ܚܪܒܐ	- Harba
Flower	ܘܪܕܐ	- Warda

Exception

Hail   ܒܪܕܐ   - Bardha

RUKAKHA ܪܘܟܟܐ In softening the letters B G D K P T only five of them follow the rule A through F. Peh is the exception. Peh is always soft when it has a semicircle under it - ܦ

NOTE: Peh is placed with the Bghadikpath group of letters because <u>Peh</u> has two sounds, hard as in <u>P</u>eter and soft as in <u>w</u>ater.

- A- When one of the five letters is non-vocalized and is preceded by a vocalized letter, it becomes soft.

  Hope   ܣܒܪܐ   - Sawra

  Reward, Wage   ܐܓܪܐ   - Aghra

- B- When one of the five letters is vocalized and is preceded by a non-vocalized letter, it becomes soft.

Neck   ܩܕܠܐ   - Qdhala

He did, made   ܥܒܕ   - Awadh

Also, when one of the five letters is vocalized and is preceded by two non-vocalized letters, it becomes soft.

Rabbit   ܐܪܢܒܐ   - Arnwa

Queen   ܡܠܟܬܐ   - Malktha

- C- When a non-vocalized Alap or Yodh are preceded by a vocalized letter but are followed by one of the five vocalized consonants, it becomes soft.

Wolf   ܕܐܒܐ   - dewa

Feast   ܥܐܕܐ   - Aedha

- D- When one of the five letters is preceded by a vocalized letter with any of the vowels except Pthaha and zlama psheeqa, it becomes soft.

Good　　　　　ܛܒܐ　　　　- Tawa

Hand　　　　　ܐܝܕܐ　　　- Eedha

Kingdom　　　ܡܠܟܘܬܐ　- Malkootha

Faith, Religion　ܗܘܕܝܬܐ　- Tawdeetha

E- When a word begins with one of the five vocalized letters and is preceded by any of the B D O L (used in nouns) or A M N T (used in verbs) it becomes soft. As an example the word for man ܓܒܪܐ and it begins with a hard gamal ܓ. But it will become soft if it follows one of the B D O L letters - ܕܓܒܪܐ dghawra (of the man). Note: The gamal ܓ - G becomes Gh. The same rule applies to the verbs - ܬܪܓܡ - targim becomes ܢܬܪܓܡ - Nthargim. Note the taw ܬ - T becomes Th.

He did　　　　ܥܒܕ　　　- Awidh

17- Punctuation: Due to the influence of foreign languages some Aramaic orthographies use the following punctuation:

A- ⁚ - a semi – colon is generally used to indicate a comma and sometimes a semi-colon

B- . – A period is generally used to indicate a full stop, interrogation, exclamation and sometimes used as a colon or comma. NOTE: In modern printed books exclamation interrogative marks are used.

C- ❖ - A diamond is generally used to indicate the end of stanzas and paragraphs.

18- The Names of the Numbers ܫܡܗܐ ܕܡܢܝܢܐ Numerals in Aramaic are nouns and are divided into two classification: Cardinal and Ordinal.

The Cardinal numbers are divided into:

A- Simple ܦܫܝܛܐ - 1 through 9 plus by tens as 20, 30, to 100.

85

Compound ܡܪܟܒܐ - 11 through 19 plus 21 through 101.

B- Masculine and feminine. The masculine number, ܚܕ and two, ܬܪܝܢ, is written without an Alap, but from three to ten the masculine numbers terminate in Alap. In contrast, the feminine number one, ܚܕܐ Ends in an Alap, but from three to ten terminate without an Alap. (Exception 8 ܬܡܢܐ)

Compound number 11 to 19 feminine plural always end in the ܪܐ while the masculine numbers ends in a non-vocalized resh.

In both masculine and feminine compound numbers (11 to 19) the smaller number precedes the larger one: ܬܪܥܣܪ twelve, ܝܒ - 12.

From 20 to 100 in both masculine and feminine the numerals always terminate with the vowel ܝ hwasa and the letter noon ܝܢ as in ܥܣܪܝܢ (20), and in contrast to the numbers 11 to 19 the larger number precedes the smaller one as in 21 - ܥܣܪܝܢ ܘܚܕ .

The Cardinal Numbers

CHART: ܟܘܢܫܐ

	(Feminine) ܢܩܒ݂ܬܢܝܐ	(Masculine) ܕܟ݂ܪܢܝܐ
One	ܚܕܐ	ܚܕ
Two	ܬܪܬܝܢ	ܬܪܝܢ
Three	ܬܠܬ	ܬܠܬܐ
Four	ܐܪܒܥ	ܐܪܒܥܐ
Five	ܚܡܫ	ܚܡܫܐ
Six	ܫܬ	ܫܬܐ

Pronounced (ܐܫܬܐ)

NOTE: (ܐܫܬܐ) See Ch. 2, rule 13:B - ܫܬܐ

Seven	ܫܒܥ	ܫܒܥܐ
Eight	ܬܡܢܐ	ܬܡܢܝܐ
Nine	ܬܫܥ	ܬܫܥܐ
Ten	ܥܣܪ	ܥܣܪܐ
Eleven	ܚܕܥܣܪܐ	ܚܕܥܣܪ
Twelve	ܬܪܬܥܣܪܐ	ܬܪܥܣܪ

Thirteen	ܬܠܬܥܣܪܐ	ܬܠܬܥܣܪ
Fourteen	ܐܪܒܥܣܪܐ	ܐܪܒܥܣܪ
Fifteen	ܚܡܫܥܣܪܐ	ܚܡܫܥܣܪ
Sixteen	ܫܬܥܣܪܐ	ܫܬܥܣܪ
(Or)	ܫܬܥܣܪܐ	
Seventeen	ܫܒܥܣܪܐ	ܫܒܥܣܪ
Eighteen	ܬܡܢܥܣܪܐ	ܬܡܢܥܣܪ
Nineteen	ܬܫܥܣܪܐ	ܬܫܥܣܪ

From twenty to one hundred the same word is used for both masculine and feminine.

Twenty	ܥܣܪܝܢ
Thirty	ܬܠܬܝܢ
Forty	ܐܪܒܥܝܢ
Fifty	ܚܡܫܝܢ
Sixty	ܫܬܝܢ
Seventy	ܫܒܥܝܢ
Eighty	ܬܡܢܝܢ
Ninety	ܬܫܥܝܢ
One hundred	ܡܐܐ

The Ordinal numbers also are either masculine or feminine.

A- Masculine ordinals are formed by adding ܝܳܐ at the end the word as in first ܩܲܕܡܵܝܵܐ

   except the ordinal second ܬܪܲܝܵܢܵܐ .

B- Feminine ordinal are formed by adding ܬܳܐ at the end of the word as in first

   ܩܲܕܡܵܝܬܵܐ Except the ordinal second ܬܪܲܝܵܢܝܬܵܐ

The Ordinal Numbers

CHART: ܠܘܚܵܐ

	Feminine	Masculine
	ܝܣܟܡܵܬܵܐ	ܕܓܢܣܵܐ
First	ܩܲܕܡܵܝܬܵܐ	ܩܲܕܡܵܝܵܐ
Second	ܬܪܲܝܵܢܝܬܵܐ	ܬܪܲܝܵܢܵܐ
Third	ܬܠܝܼܬܵܝܬܵܐ	ܬܠܝܼܬܵܝܵܐ
Fourth	ܪܒ݂ܝܼܥܵܝܬܵܐ	ܪܒ݂ܝܼܥܵܝܵܐ
Fifth	ܚܡܝܼܫܵܝܬܵܐ	ܚܡܝܼܫܵܝܵܐ
Six	ܫܬܝܼܬܵܝܬܵܐ	ܫܬܝܼܬܵܝܵܐ
Seventh	ܫܒ݂ܝܼܥܵܝܬܵܐ	ܫܒ݂ܝܼܥܵܝܵܐ
Eighth	ܬܡܝܼܢܵܝܬܵܐ	ܬܡܝܼܢܵܝܵܐ
Ninth	ܬܫܝܼܥܵܝܬܵܐ	ܬܫܝܼܥܵܝܵܐ
Tenth	ܥܣܝܼܪܵܝܬܵܐ	ܥܣܝܼܪܵܝܵܐ

Eleventh	ܚܕܥܣܝܪܬܐ	ܚܕܥܣܝܪܝܐ
Twelfth	ܬܪܥܣܝܪܬܐ	ܬܪܥܣܝܪܝܐ
Thirteenth	ܬܠܬܥܣܝܪܬܐ	ܬܠܬܥܣܝܪܝܐ
Fourteenth	ܐܪܒܥܣܝܪܬܐ	ܐܪܒܥܣܝܪܝܐ
Fifteenth	ܚܡܫܥܣܝܪܬܐ	ܚܡܫܥܣܝܪܝܐ
Sixteenth	ܫܬܥܣܝܪܬܐ	ܫܬܥܣܝܪܝܐ
Seventeenth	ܫܒܥܣܝܪܬܐ	ܫܒܥܣܝܪܝܐ
Eighteenth	ܬܡܢܥܣܝܪܬܐ	ܬܡܢܥܣܝܪܝܐ
Nineteenth	ܬܫܥܣܝܪܬܐ	ܬܫܥܣܝܪܝܐ
Twentieth	ܥܣܪܝܢܝܬܐ	ܥܣܪܝܢܝܐ
Thirtieth	ܬܠܬܝܢܝܬܐ	ܬܠܬܝܢܝܐ
Fortieth	ܐܪܒܥܝܢܝܬܐ	ܐܪܒܥܝܢܝܐ
Fiftieth	ܚܡܫܝܢܝܬܐ	ܚܡܫܝܢܝܐ
Sixtieth	ܫܬܝܢܝܬܐ	ܫܬܝܢܝܐ
Seventieth	ܫܒܥܝܢܝܬܐ	ܫܒܥܝܢܝܐ
Eightieth	ܬܡܢܝܢܝܬܐ	ܬܡܢܝܢܝܐ
Ninetieth	ܬܫܥܝܢܝܬܐ	ܬܫܥܝܢܝܐ

One hundredth and one thousandth are not used in Aramaic. The cardinal number is used.

Intermediary ordinal numbers from twenty to one hundred are formed by joining the ordinals of the units to those of the tens by the conjunction ܘ , as ܗܠܡܝܢܝܬ݂ ܕܚܕܟܣܪܝܬ݂ - 25th, ܝܗܕܣܪܝܬ݂ ܘܣܩܒܝܥܝܬ݂ - 31st, ܘܬܪܝܢܝܬ݂ ܘܐܪܒܥܝܢܝܬ݂ – 42nd, etc.

The numbers one (1) to four hundred (400) correspond to the 22 letters of the Aramaic alphabet. (See Chapter One). The letters ܐ through ܛ are the single numbers 1 – 9.

Beginning with ܝ (10) each succeeding letter is counted by tens until ܩ (100).

Beginning with ܩ (100) each succeeding letter is counted by hundreds until ܬ (400)

The last number to be counted in this method is 499 ܬܨܛ.

There are two methods employed to count from 500 to 999:

A- The following method is used by some Aramaic grammarians and in the majority of liturgical books and is the most common method:

$$ܬ + ܩ = 500 - ܬܩ$$

$$ܬ + ܬ + ܩ = 900 - ܬܬܩ$$

ܬܩܟܐ =521 . ܬܩܗ = 605 . ܬܩܨܛ = 799

ܬܬܩܨܛ = 999 . ܬܬܩܛ = 899 .

B- The second method which is employed by other grammarians is as follows:
Beginning at 100 to 999 each letter from ܝ to ܨ represents 100 when a dot is placed above the letter.

91

900 = ܨ . 400 = ܬܼ . 100 = ܩܼ

999 = ܨܛܨ . 545 = ܩܡܗ . 122 = ܩܟܒ

(Qop, Resh, Sheen and Taw ܩܪܫܬ are not included).

Alap is the cardinal numeral 1, but when alap stands alone and a slanted line is placed beneath it ܐ , it equals one thousands (1,000). When a small horizontal line is placed beneath it ܐ, it equals ten thousands (10.000). But when two slanted lines joined at the top are placed beneath that alap ܐ, it equals one hundred thousand (100,000).

In a four digit number, as in 1989, the following method is employed:

A- When the numerals Alap through Sade are the second number of a four digit number, each one counts as a thousands, that is, ܐ is 1,000, ܒ is 2,000, etc. until ܛ which is 9,000.

B- When the numerals Yodh through Sade are the second number of a four digit number, each one counts as a hundred, that is, ܝ is 100, ܟ is 200 etc. until ܨ which is 900.

C- The third numeral of the four digit number remains unchanged from the basic method ܝ (10) through ܨ (90) is counted by tens. And for the final digit the basic method ܐ (1) and ܛ (9) is followed.

Thus the year 1989 is ܐܛܦܛ

It reads as follows:

ܐܠܦ ܘܬܫܥܡܐܐ ܘܬܡܢܝܢ ܘܬܫܥܐ

Also, the year 2154 is ܒܩܢܕ

It reads as follows;

ܬܪܝܢ ܐܠܦܝܢ ܘܡܐܐ ܘܚܡܫܝܢ ܘܐܪܒܥܐ

1990 is ܐܛܦܨ

CHAPTER THREE

NOUNS AND ADJECTIVES

CHAPTER THREE
NOUNS AND ADJECTIVES

Reading

ܐ. ܓܒܪܐ ܕܡܠܟܐ ܐܝܬܘܗܝ ܟܐܢܐ.

ܒ. ܐܒܐ ܘܒܪܐ ܐܝܬܝܗܘܢ ܒܪܝ.

ܓ. ܐܡܚܠܐ ܕܐܢܬܬܐ.

ܕ. ܝܠܕܐ ܕܛܠܝܬܐ.

ܗ. ܐܒܗܐ ܘܐܚ̈ܐ.

ܘ. ܒܬ̈ܐ ܘܒܝܬܐ.

ܙ. ܗܘܘ ܐܢܫ̈ܐ ܘܒܟ̈ܐ.

ܚ. ܥܠ ܕܐܢܬܬܐ ܐܝܬܘܗܝ ܒܪܝܬܐ.

ܛ. ܗܘܡܢܐ ܘܚܟܡܐ ܐܝܬܘܗܝ ܚܝܐ.

ܝ. ܚܕܐ ܕܐܢܬܬܐ ܐܝܬܘܗܝ ܟܐܢܐ ܘܒܪܝܬܐ.

VOCABULARY

Nouns

Father, Fathers   ܐܒܐ . ܐܒܗ̈ܐ

Woman, Women, Wife, Wives   ܐܢܬܬܐ . ܢܫ̈ܐ

House, Houses   ܒܝܬܐ . ܒ̈ܬܐ

Son, sons	ܒܪܐ . ܒܢ̈ܝܐ
Daughter, Daughters	(ܒܪܬ) ܒܪܬܐ . ܒܢ̈ܬܐ
Temple	ܗܝܟܠܐ ܗܝܟ̈ܠܐ
Dream	ܚܠܡܐ ܚܠ̈ܡܐ
Boy, Boys	ܛܠܝܐ . ܛܠ̈ܝܐ
Girl, Girls	ܛܠܝܬܐ . ܛܠܝ̈ܬܐ
Book	ܟܬܒܐ ܟܬ̈ܒܐ
Queen, Queens	ܡܠܟܬܐ . ܡܠ̈ܟܬܐ
Mare, Mares	ܣܘܣܬܐ . ܣܘܣ̈ܝܬܐ
Name, Names	ܫܡܐ . ܫܡ̈ܗܐ

Adjectives

Black - M S & M P	ܐܘܟܡܐ . ܐܘܟ̈ܡܐ
Black - F S & F P	ܐܘܟܡܬܐ . ܐܘܟ̈ܡܬܐ
Nice, Sweet - M S & M P	ܒܣܝܡܐ . ܒܣܝ̈ܡܐ
Nice, Sweet - F S & F P	ܒܣܝܡܬܐ . ܒܣܝ̈ܡܬܐ
White - M S & M P	ܚܘܪܐ . ܚܘ̈ܪܐ
White - F S & F P	ܚܘܪܬܐ . ܚܘ̈ܪܬܐ

Good - F S & F P	ܛܵܒ݂ܬܵܐ . ܛܵܒ݂ܵܬܹܐ
Small - M S & M P	ܙܥܘܿܪܵܐ . ܙܥܘܿܪܹܐ
Small - F S & F P	ܙܥܘܿܪܬܵܐ . ܙܥܘܿܪܵܬܹܐ
Pious, Just - M S & M P	ܙܲܕܝܼܩܵܐ . ܙܲܕܝܼܩܹܐ
Pious, Just - F S & F P	ܙܲܕܝܼܩܬܵܐ . ܙܲܕܝܼܩܵܬܹܐ
Humble, Meek - M S & M P	ܡܲܟ݂ܝܼܟ݂ܵܐ . ܡܲܟ݂ܝܼܟ݂ܹܐ
Humble, Meek - F S & F P	ܡܲܟ݂ܝܼܟ݂ܬܵܐ . ܡܲܟ݂ܝܼܟ݂ܵܬܹܐ
Red - M S & M P	ܣܘܼܡܵܩܵܐ . ܣܘܼܡܵܩܹܐ
Red - F S & F P	ܣܘܼܡܵܩܬܵܐ . ܣܘܼܡܵܩܵܬܹܐ
Holy - M S & M P	ܩܲܕܝܼܫܵܐ . ܩܲܕܝܼܫܹܐ
Holy - F S & F P	ܩܲܕܝܼܫܬܵܐ . ܩܲܕܝܼܫܵܬܹܐ
Big, Great, Large - M S & M P	ܪܵܒܵܐ ܪܲܒܵܐ . ܪܵܘܪܒܹܐ
Big, Great, Large - F S & F P	ܪܲܒܬܵܐ . ܪܵܘܪܒܼܵܬܹܐ
Beautiful - M S & M P	ܫܲܦܝܼܪܵܐ . ܫܲܦܝܼܪܹܐ
Beautiful - F S & F P	ܫܲܦܝܼܪܬܵܐ . ܫܲܦܝܼܪܵܬܹܐ

Verbs

He, it is	ܐܝܼܬܼܵܘܗܝ
They are	ܐܝܼܬܲܝܗܘܿܢ

Nouns ܫܡܗܐ in Aramaic are either primitive or derivative. Primitive nouns cannot be traced to any other word. Derivative nouns are derived from other words - verbs.

Nouns are grouped:

Substantive ܡܫܬܡܗܢܐ

Adjective ܫܡܗܐ

A substantive (noun) indicates a person, place, thing, quality or event.

Examples:

Simon Peter ܫܡܥܘܢ ܟܐܦܐ

Man ܓܒܪܐ

Bethlehem ܒܝܬ ܠܚܡ

Heart ܠܒܐ

An adjective modifies a noun, that is, tells something about the noun: A black (adj.) horse (noun).

NOTE: In Aramaic the noun comes before the adjective – A horse black.

(Reminder: Read from right to left in Aramaic) ܣܘܣܝܐ ܐܘܟܡܐ

Note: The word, singular and plural, for noun is: ܫܡܗܐ ܫܡܐ

The word singular and plural, for verb is: ܡܠܬܐ ܡܠܐ

Examples

Big, Great ܪܒܐ

Beautiful ܫܦܝܪܐ

A big horse   ܣܘܣܝܐ ܪܒܐ

Nouns and Adjectives agree in 1) Gender 2) Number:

1- Gender ܓܢܣܐ in Aramaic most word are classified as either

    Masculine ܕܟܪܢܝܐ or Feminine ܢܩܒܬܢܝܐ

Nouns and Adjectives

Masculine Singular	Feminine Singular
ܝܠܕܐ ܛܒܐ	ܝܠܕܬܐ ܛܒܬܐ
ܣܘܣܝܐ ܣܝܦܐ	ܣܘܣܬܐ ܣܝܦܬܐ
ܟܠܒܐ ܕܐܒܐ	ܐܝܡܗܐ ܥܩܝܕܬܐ
ܣܠܩܐ ܒܘܪܟܐ	ܝܠܦܗܐ ܚܒܝܫܬܐ

NOTE: Singular masculine nouns and adjectives usually end in Zqapa and Alap ܐ (See above masculine examples).

    Males, their names and status, names of rivers, mountains, hills, peoples and months of the year are masculine in gender.

    Singular feminine nouns and adjectives usually end in Taw, Zqapa, and Alap. There are some singular feminine adjectives that end in soft Taw, Zqapa and Alap (See above feminine examples).

    Females, their names and status, names of countries, regions, cities, towns, islands, the four corners of the earth, particles, letters of the alphabet, and members of the body in pairs such as eye ܥܝܢܐ, hand ܐܝܕܐ are feminine in gender. Exceptions: arms, breast. (All other members of the human body and internal organs are masculine).

2- Number ܡܢܝܢܐ Nouns and Adjectives are either:

    Singular ܚܕܢܝܐ or Plural ܣܓܝܐܢܝܐ

Rules for forming the plural masculine and feminine nouns and adjectives:

A- Masculine words usually end in Zqapa and Alap ܐܳ   To make the words plural, Zqapa ܳ changes to Zlama qashya ܶ and a syame ̈ is placed above one of the appropriate letters.

Examples: temple ܗܰܝܟܠܐ changes to ܗܰܝܟ̈ܠܶܐ temples and good ܛܳܒܳܐ changes to ܛܳܒܶ̈ܐ (The adjective "good" does not become plural in English).

NOTE: There are some irregular masculine nouns and adjectives in the plural form.

B- When an adjective begins with a vocalized letter which carries a Pthaha ܰ and ends with a yodh Alap ܝܐ , the Pthaha ܰ moves from the first letter to the second.

Example: blind ܣܰܡܝܐ (pl.). ܣܡܰܝ̈ܐ

If the first letter has a Zqapa ܳ and end with a Yodh Alap ܝܐ, the second letter takes a Pthaha ܰ

Examples: lost ܛܳܠܝܐ (pl) ܛܠܰܝ̈ܐ

C- When a word is in two syllables and ends with Taw Alap ܬܐ , the non-vocalized letter which precedes Taw takes a Zqapa ܳ
Examples:
Image ܨܘܪܬܐ (pl) ܨܘܪ̈ܬܐ
Friday ܥܪܘܒܬܐ (pl) ܥܪ̈ܘܒܬܐ

D- When a word has three or four syllables and ends in Taw Alap ܬܐ , the non-vocalized letter which precedes Taw ܬ takes a Zqapa ܳ and the letter which comes before the one which just took the Zqapa ܳ will become a non-vocalized letter.

Examples: Knowledge ܝܕܰܥܬܐ (pl) ܝܕܰܥ̈ܬܐ

E- Feminine words usually end in Taw, Zqapa and Alap ܬܐ and there are some words in the singular that will end in soft Taw, Zqapa and Alap ܬܐ to make the words plural

the letter which precedes the Taw will take a Zqapa and the Taw is softened ܬܳ݁
and a Syame is placed above one of the appropriate letters.

Examples:

Queen ܡܲܠܟܬܳܐ changes to ܡܲܠܟܳܬ̈ܳܐ queens and evil ܒܝܼܫܬܳܐ changes to ܒܝܼܫܳܬ̈ܳܐ

NOTE: There are some irregular feminine nouns and adjectives in the plural form.

Masculine   **Feminine**
Plural   Plural

ܐܒ̈ܗܐ ܐܒܐ   ܐܬ̈ܬܐ ܐܢܬܬܐ

ܐܚܘ̈ܢܐ ܐܚܐ   ܐܚܘ̈ܬܐ ܚܬܐ

ܠܝܘ̈ܬܐ ܒܪܐ   ܒܢ̈ܬܐ ܒܪܬܐ

ܫܠܡܐ ܫܢ̈ܝܐ   ܫܢ̈ܬܐ ܡܫܢ̈ܝܬܐ

3- State ܓܕܡܐ (literally "cutting off" or a "contraction").

The Gdhama is formed by deleting one or two letters and changing one or more vowels at the end of a word.

Examples:

Book ܟܬܳܒܳܐ contracted - ܟܬܒ   Village ܩܪܝܬܐ Contracted - ܩܪܝ

House of bread ܒܝܬܐ or ܒܝܬ and ܠܚܡܐ contracted ܒܝܬܠܚܡ

There are three states of a noun in Aramaic: 1) Emphatic, 2) Construct and 3) Absolute. The most commonly used state is the emphatic state (sometimes called definite) such as man ܓܒܪܐ Since there are no definite or indefinite articles in Aramaic, some grammarians suggest that the emphatic form of a word implies a definite or indefinite article.

The construct state ܓܕܡܐ ܒܢܝܢܐ is only used when one noun depends on another.

Examples: King of Kings - ܡܠܟ ܡܠܟܐ .

The absolute state ܟܬܒܐ ܩܕܝܫܐ is the simplest form of a noun when it stands alone

King - ܡܠܟ

REVIEW

1- Translate the following phrase into Aramaic in the singular form.

1) The holy book. _____

2) The good man. _____

3) The good woman. _____

4) The bad boy. _____

5) The bad girl. _____

6) The great king. _____

7) The beautiful queen. _____

8) The black horse. _____

9) The white mare. _____

10) The holy man. _____

11) The bad son. _____

12) The humble daughter. _____

13) A bad dream. _____

14) The small house. _____

15) The big temple. _____

16) Great peace. _____

17) A nice name. _____

18) The holy God. _____

19) The good God. _____

20) The pious father. _____

2- Translate the above phrase into Aramaic in plural form.

1) _____ .
2) _____ .
3) _____ .
4) _____ .
5) _____ .
6) _____ .
7) _____ .
8) _____ .
9) _____ .
10) _____ .
11) _____ .
12) _____ .
13) _____ .
14) _____ .
15) _____ .
16) _____ .
17) _____ .
18) _____ .

19) _____ .

20) _____ .

3- Translate the following Aramaic sentences into English.

ܐ. ܐܝܚܠܐ ܘܟܘܬܐ.

ܐ. _____

ܒ. ܓܒܪܐ ܚܝܐ.

ܒ. _____

ܓ. ܡܠܟܐ ܘܚܟܝܡܐ.

ܓ. _____

ܕ. ܐܒܗܬܐ ܥܒܝܕܬܐ.

ܕ. _____

ܗ. ܡܠܟܬܐ ܚܝܬܐ.

ܗ. _____

ܘ. ܗܘܝܬ ܚܝܬܐ.

ܘ. _____

ܙ. ܗܘܬ ܪܒܬܐ.

ܙ. _____

܁. ܟܳܬܒܳܐ ܗܘܦܟܝܬܳܐ.

܁. ‎_____

ܒ. ܟܬܳܒܳܐ ܚܕܬܳܐ.

ܒ. ‎_____

܁. ܒܰܝܬܳܐ ܪܰܒܳܐ.

܁. ‎_____

܁. ܐܰܬܬܳܐ ܒܰܣܝܡܬܳܐ.

܁. ‎_____

ܗ. ܐܰܒܪܳܐ ܛܳܒܳܐ.

ܗ. ‎_____

CHAPTER FOUR

INSEPARABLE PREPOSITIONS

CHAPTER FOUR
INSEPARABLE PREPOSITIONS

Reading

ܐ. ܓܡܠܐ ܕܐܒܐ ܕܢܘܗܒ.

ܒ. ܗܐ ܕܘܝܕ ܕܡܚܕܐ ܐܠܗܐ ܕܒܓܘܗܝ ܒܝܬ ܡܥܒܝܢܐ.

ܓ. ܚܠܒܐ ܒܝܕ ܓܡܠܐ.

ܕ. ܒܝܘܡܐ ܕܒܓܘܗܝ ܕܬܪܝܢܐ.

ܗ. ܒܘܕܐ ܕܡܥܒܝܢܐ.

ܘ. ܬܠܐ ܕܢܦܫܐ.

ܙ. ܡܝܠܢܐ ܝܘܕܗܐ.

ܚ. ܗܐ ܡܥܒܝܢܐ ܕܒܓܘܗܝ ܠܗܡ ܡܚܕܐ ܐܠܗܐ.

ܛ. ܫܠܚܐ ܕܓܡܠܐ ܠܒܗܗܝ ܚܡܝܦܐ.

ܝ. ܚܠ ܕܘܝܕ ܕܡܝ ܐܠܗܐ.

VOCABULARY

1- Camel	ܓܡܠܐ
2- Behold	ܗܐ
3- Milk	ܚܠܒܐ

4- Joseph ܝܘܣܦ

5- Sea ܝܲܡܵܐ

6- All ܟܠ

7- Dog ܟܲܠܒܵܐ

8- To, with, toward, beside ܠܘܵܬ

9- Salt ܡܸܠܚܵܐ

10- From ܡܸܢ

11- Lord God ܡܵܪܝܵܐ ܐܲܠܵܗܵܐ

12- Messiah, Christ ܡܫܝܼܚܵܐ

13- Fish ܢܘܼܢܵܐ

14- Fire ܢܘܼܪܵܐ

15- On, upon, over ܥܲܠ

16- With ܥܲܡ

17- Voice ܩܵܠܵܐ

18- Wind, Spirit ܪܘܼܚܵܐ

THE INSEPARABLE PREPOSITIONS ܡܲܦܠܲܬܼܵܐ (See p. 73, Ch. 2 – rule 4)

Maplatha means prefixes and they are the four letters BDOL (Bdhol).

B ܒ - in, by, at, with, through, by means of

D ܕ - of, from

O ܘ - and

L ܠ - to, for

110

They are called inseparable prepositions, or particles, because they are prefixed to a noun. (A particle is a word that cannot be inflected, that is, change form, such as a preposition, conjunction, article, or interjection). Of the four letters ܠ ܘ ܕ ܒ , only ܕ and ܘ may be prefixed to a verb.

Examples:

To work   ܥܒܕ

That he works   ܕܥܒܕ

And he works   ܘܥܒܕ

NOTE: The letter ܕ is also used as a relative pronoun (that, which, who, whom, and whose) and it introduces a relative clause. The letter ܘ is used as a conjunction - and.

Rules: In Aramaic the first letter of a noun or a word is either vocalized or non-vocalized and affects the inseparable prepositions.

    A- Non-vocalized: When the initial letter of a noun is non-vocalized, the BDOL letters must be vocalized with a Pthaha ◌ܰ

Examples: Book ܟܬܒܐ , in the book ܒܟܬܒܐ

     When two BDOL letters are prefixed to a non-vocalized letter, only the second BDOL letter takes a Pthaha ◌ܰ

Example: Book ܟܬܒܐ , and for the book ܘܠܟܬܒܐ

    B- Vocalized: When the initial letter of a noun is vocalized, the BDOL letters are written without a vowel.

Example: House ܒܝܬܐ , to the house ܠܒܝܬܐ

When two BDOL letters are prefixed to a vocalized letter, the first BDOL letter takes a Pthaha ◌̇

Example: House ܒܝܬܐ , that which is to the house ܠܒܝܬܐ

C- Initial Alap: When the initial letter of a noun has a vocalized or non-vocalized Alap, the BDOL letters take the sound of the Alap.

Example: Vocalized ܐ̇ : God ܐܠܗܐ in God ܒܐܠܗܐ balaha.

Non-Vocalized ܐ : man ܐܢܫܐ , in man ܒܐܢܫܐ bnasha.

Note: When used in front of one of the BDOL letters, the Alap in Jesus, ܝܫܘܥ is removed.

Ex. ܕܝܫܘܥ

REVIEW

1- Translate the following phrase into Aramaic.

  1) God's temple. _____

  2) The king's horse. _____

  3) The queen is in the house. _____

  4) The peace of God. _____

  5) The man and the woman. _____

  6) God's holy book. _____

  7) In the name of the father. _____

  8) The father's beautiful daughter. _____

  9) Behold, peace to the house. _____

  10) The spirit of God is upon the water. _____

  11) And to God who is in the temple. _____

12) Of the king, for the king. _____

13) To the king, by the king. _____

14) Through the king, from the king. _____

2- Translate the following Aramaic sentences into English.

ܐ. ܫܡܵܐ ܕܡܲܠܟܵܐ.

_____

ܒ. ܫܠܵܡܵܐ ܕܐܲܪܥܵܐ.

_____

ܓ. ܗܘܸܡܵܢ ܣܘܼܣܵܐ ܕܡܸܠܟܵܐ.

_____

ܕ. ܚܙܵܬܹܐ ܥܲܒܕܵܐ ܕܒܹܕܵܐ.

_____

ܗ. ܘܕܸܠܡܸܕܵܐ.

_____

ܘ. ܐܝܼܬ ܡܕܝܼܢܬܵܐ ܕܒܹܕܵܐ ܚܕܵܐ.

_____

ܙ. ܟܬܵܒܵܐ ܕܐܲܒܵܗܵܬܹܐ ܕܙܕܝܼܩܘܼܬܼ ܫܒܼܝܼܚܬܵܐ ܘܥܵܒܼܕܵܬܹܐ.

_____

ܣ. ܥܠܩܐ ܠܡܠܚܡܐ ܘܠܡܠܟܐ.

ܗܕ. ܥܩܐ ܚܒܥܐ ܕܟܕܢܐ.

ܒܙ. ܒܝܬܐ ܕܡܠܟܐ ܫܚܝܩܐ.

ܚܒ. ܘܒܢܬܐ ܕܒܘܣܟܐ.

ܡܚ. ܐܘ ܕܘܢܐ ܕܡܩܕܢܐ ܒܝܬܐ ܒܝܕ ܒܩܐ.

CHAPTER FIVE

PERSONAL PRONOUNS AND PRONOMINAL SUFFIXES

CHAPTER FIVE
PERSONAL PRONOUNS AND PRONOMINAL SUFFIXES

Reading

ܐ. ܫܿܡܝ ܗܘܼܝܘ ܕܡܘܼܫܹܐ.

ܒ. ܥܠܝܼܡܹܐ ܗܿܕܹܐ ܗܘܼܘܵܗܿ ܚܕܵܐ ܘܿܡܫܹܐ ܠܓܲܒܼܪܵܐ.

ܓ. ܚܕܵܢܵܐ ܕܲܗܒܼܵܐ ܡܸܠܟܵܐ ܠܥܸܠ ܡܥܒܼܝܼܢܵܐ ܩܕܘܿܡܿܗܵ.

ܕ. ܡܵܕܼܒܸܿܐ ܘܕܼܘܼܢܼܘܿ ܕܘܲܠܿܢܵ ܠܿܡܵ ܫܿܡܝ.

ܗ. ܡܥܒܼܝܼܢܵܐ ܗܿܕܹܐ ܘܩܕܘܿܡܿܗܵ.

ܘ. ܐܸܢܵܐ ܐܼܢܵܐ ܗܿܕܹܐ ܕܒܼܹܬܼܵܐ.

ܙ. ܡܸܠܲܚ ܕܲܗܒܼܵܐ: ܐܸܢܵܐ ܐܼܢܵܐ ܡܥܒܼܝܼܢܵܐ.

ܚ. ܡܸܠܟܿܒܼܵܗܿ ܚܕܵܐ ܓܲܒܼܵܐ ܕܲܙܲܟܼܵܗܿ.

ܛ. ܓܿܕܸܐ ܕܼܒܼܘܿܗܼܘܲܣ ܓܲܠܒܼܵܐ.

ܝ. ܡܸܠܓܝܹܗ ܚܿܡܼܕܼ ܕܸܓܼܒܼܵܿܬܼܵ.

VOCABULARY

1- Went ܙܝܠ

2- (They) Went ܙܝܠܗ

3- Said ܐܡܪ

4- Built ܒܢܐ

5- Walked ܗܠܟ

6- Priest ܟܗܢܐ

7- Wrote ܟܬܒ

8- Word, words ܡܠܬܐ، ܡܠܐ

9- Lord ܡܪܝܐ

10- Mary ܡܪܝܡ

11- People ܥܡܐ

12- Savior ܦܪܘܩܐ

13- Thomas ܬܐܘܡܐ

THE PRONOUN AND ITS DIVISIONS ܫܡܐ ܥܡܐ ܘܦܘܠܓܘܗܝ

Personal, demonstrative, interrogative, indefinite, and pronominal suffix.
A pronoun is a word which takes the place of a noun. It is divided into two groups:

1- Separate (Subject) pronoun: ܫܡܐ ܥܡܐ ܡܦܪܫܐ

Subject pronouns come before a noun and stand alone. There are ten personal pronouns:

FIRST PERSON   (TWO PRONOUNS)

M and F Singular   I   ܐܢܐ

M and F Plural   We   ܚܢܢ

SECOND PERSON (Four pronouns)

Masculine Singular   You   ܐܢܬ

Feminine Singular   You   ܐܢܬܝ

Masculine Plural   You   ܐܢܬܘܢ

Feminine Plural   You   ܐܢܬܝܢ

THIRD PERSON (Four pronouns)

Masculine Singular   He   ܗܘ

Feminine Singular   She   ܗܝ

Masculine Plural   They   ܗܢܘܢ

Feminine Plural   They   ܗܢܝܢ

NOTE: In Aramaic the first and second person singular sometimes doubles to indicate:

I am and you are.

I am   ܐܢܐ ܐܢܐ

You are   ܐܢܬ ܐܢܬܝ

This form emphasizes the essence of being and, at times, is used in place of the verb – to be.

   A- Write each subject pronoun five times.

     1) _____ _____ _____ _____ _____
     2) _____ _____ _____ _____ _____

3) _____ _____ _____ _____ _____ _____
4) _____ _____ _____ _____ _____ _____
5) _____ _____ _____ _____ _____ _____
6) _____ _____ _____ _____ _____ _____
7) _____ _____ _____ _____ _____ _____
8) _____ _____ _____ _____ _____ _____
9) _____ _____ _____ _____ _____ _____
10) _____ _____ _____ _____ _____ _____

B- Identify the following pronouns in English.

_____ ܐܢܘܢ

_____ ܐܢܝܢ

_____ ܗܘ

_____ ܗܝ

_____ ܐܢܬܘܢ

_____ ܐܢܬܝܢ

_____ ܗܘ

_____ ܐܢܐ

_____ ܐܢܬ

_____ ܐܢܬܝ

2- Suffixed (Inseparable) pronounce:
   Inseparable pronouns are attached (suffixed) to verbs and nouns.
   Examples – Verbs:

   He made   ܥܒܕ

   She made   ܥܒܕܗ

You made   ܥܒ݂ܕܗ

NOTE: The letter Taw ܬ is suffixed at the end of the verb to indicate she or you.

Examples – Nouns:

Son – ܒܪܐ and beloved - ܚܒܝܒܐ

My son - ܒܪܝ and my beloved - ܚܒܝܒܝ

NOTE: The letter yodh ܝ is suffixed to son and beloved.

PRONOMINAL SUFFIXES (Possessive Pronouns).
There are ten possessive pronouns and Aramaic grammarians formed them in a word

ܓܗܘܒܢ -

King   ܡܠܟܐ

First Person

M and F Singular	My king	(ܝ)	ܡܠܟܝ
M and F Plural	Our king	(ܢ݁ܝ)	ܡܠܟܢ

Second Person

M Singular	Your king	(ܟ݁)	ܡܠܟܟ
F Singular	Your king	(ܟ݁ܝ)	ܡܠܟܟܝ
M Plural	Your king	(ܟܘܢ)	ܡܠܟܟܘܢ
F Plural	Your king	(ܟܝܢ)	ܡܠܟܟܝܢ

Third Person

M Singular	His king	(ܗ)	ܡܠܟܗ
F Singular	Her king	(ܗ̇)	ܡܠܟܗ̇

M Plural	Their king	(ܗܘܢ)	ܡܠܟܗܘܢ
F Plural	Their king	(ܗܝܢ)	ܡܠܟܗܝܢ

Suffixes are added to stems which are mostly formed by dropping the final Alap and the vowel preceding it - ܐ . The same rule applies to plural nouns with soft Taw – Zqapa and Alap - ܬܐ

Examples: Lord - ܡܪܐ , Lords - ܡܪܘܬܐ

When the noun is plural and has no Taw-Zqapa and Alap, ܬܐ , as in kings ܡܠܟܐ the noun is inflected as follows:

First Person

M and F Singular	My kings	(ܰܝ)	ܡܠܟܝ
M and F Plural	Our kings	(ܰܝܢ)	ܡܠܟܝܢ

Second Person

M Singular	Your kings	(ܰܝܟ)	ܡܠܟܝܟ
F Singular	Your kings	(ܰܝܟܝ)	ܡܠܟܝܟܝ
M Plural	Your kings	(ܰܝܟܘܢ)	ܡܠܟܝܟܘܢ
F Plural	Your kings	(ܰܝܟܝܢ)	ܡܠܟܝܟܝܢ

Third Person

M Singular	His kings	(ܰܘܗܝ)	ܡܠܟܘܗܝ
F Singular	Her kings	(ܶܝܗ)	ܡܠܟܝܗ
M Plural	Their kings	(ܰܝܗܘܢ)	ܡܠܟܝܗܘܢ
F Plural	Their kings	(ܰܝܗܝܢ)	ܡܠܟܝܗܝܢ

REVIEW

1- Translate the following sentences into Aramaic.

1) My king wrote in the book.

2) My boy walked to the temple.

3) His little girl walked to the house.

4) Behold, the good people built the holy temple of God.

5) I am the Savior.

6) The priest said, "Peace upon the people."

7) Jesus said, "I am the Word of God."

8) The Lord God said, "You are my son."

9) The apostle Thomas went to the temple and said to the king, "Peace."

10) The Savior wrote the words of the spirit in God's holy book.

11) I am their king and lord.

12) My kings are good and they are holy men.

13) He is a man of God.
_____

14) You are my lords!
_____

2- Translate the following sentences into English.

ܐ. ܐܢܐ ܐܢܐ ܥܒܕܐ ܕܐܠܗܐ.

1. _____

ܒ. ܡܠܦܢܘܗܝ ܛܒܝܢ.

2. _____

ܓ. ܬܠܡܝܕܘܗܝ ܒܝܫܐ.

3. _____

ܕ. ܚܒܪܘܗܝ ܪܒܐ.

4. _____

ܗ. ܡܠܟܘܗܝ ܒܝܫܐ ܠܥܡܐ.

5. _____

ܗ. ܢܩܘܡܘܢ ܕܟܒܪܐ.

ܗ. _____

ܘ. ܗܘܦܝܚܘܢ ܗܘܡܬܢܐ.

ܘ. _____

ܚ. ܦܕܘܢܝ ܘܡܠܟܝ.

ܚ. _____

ܛ. ܢܢܐ ܐܝܢܐ ܕܘܝܚܟܐ.

ܛ. _____

ܝ. ܥܠܝܗܝ ܕܝܥܩܘܕ.

ܝ. _____

CHAPTER SIX

DEMONSRTATIVE AND INTERROGATIVE PRONOUNS

CHAPTER SIX

DEMONSTRATIVE AND INTERROGATIVE PRONOUNS

Reading

ܐ. ܒܐܝܡܡܐ ܘܒܠܠܝܐ.

ܒ. ܛܘܒܐ ܗܢܐ.

ܓ. ܠܚܡܐ ܕܝܘܡ ܣܘܢܩܢܢ.

ܕ. ܦܐܪܐ ܕܐܝܠܢܐ ܐܝܬܘܗܝ ܗܢܐ.

ܗ. ܐܡܪܐ ܗܠܟ ܒܐܪܥܐ.

ܘ. ܐܝܟܘ ܠܚܡܐ ܒܒܝܬܐ.

ܙ. ܐܝܠܢܐ ܗܢܐ ܐܝܬܘܗܝ ܒܐܪܥܐ ܫܘܡܡܬܐ.

VOCABULARY

1- Tree ܐܝܠܢܐ

2- Daytime ܐܝܡܡܐ

3- Mother, Mothers ܐܡܐ: ܐܡܗܬܐ

4- Lamb ܐܡܪܐ

5- Earth ܐܪܥܐ

6- You created ܒܪܝܬ

7-	Time	ܥܕܢܐ
8-	Mountain	ܛܘܪܐ
9-	Day (24 hrs.)	ܝܘܡܐ
10-	Bread	ܠܚܡܐ
11-	Night	ܠܠܝܐ
12-	Let there be	ܢܗܘܐ
13-	Fruit	ܦܐܪܐ
14-	Door	ܬܪܥܐ

1) **Demonstrative Pronouns:** ܟܢܘܝܐ ܕܩܢܘܡܐ ܡܚܘܝܢܝܐ

There are 11 demonstrative pronouns and they are divided into two classifications: Near and Distant.

A. NEAR

Masculine Singular	this	ܗܢܐ
Feminine Singular	this	ܗܕܐ
M and F Plural	these	ܗܠܝܢ
Masculine Singular	that	ܗܘ
Feminine Singular	that	ܗܝ
Masculine Plural	these	ܗܢܘܢ
Feminine Plural	these	ܗܢܝܢ

B. DISTANT

Masculine Singular	that	ܗܘ
Feminine Singular	that	ܗܝ
Masculine Plural	those	ܗܢܘܢ
Feminine Plural	those	ܗܢܝܢ

2) **Interrogative Pronouns:** Who and Which

Masculine Singular	ܐܝܢܐ
Feminine Singular	ܐܝܕܐ
Masculine & Feminine Plural	ܐܝܠܝܢ

All three above are used for persons and things.

What, how - ܡܢܘ ، ܡܐ ، ܡܢܐ are used for things regardless of gender or number.

How many - ܟܡܐ is used for people and things regardless of number and gender.

The Aramaic word "how many" is a combination of the letter ܟ (much) and the word "how" - ܡܐ

NOTE: Who is, what is, which is (used for persons or things) may be contracted ܐܝܢܘ
This contraction is a combination of ܐܝܢܐ and ܗܘ. The same contraction occurs with – who is it ܡܢܘ. This word is a combination of ܡܢ and ܗܘ. The same rule applies for what is it ܡܢܘ. This word is a combination of ܡܢܐ and ܗܘ.

A relative pronoun ܡܢ ܕܐܡܪ occurs when the interrogative is followed by a Dalath which precedes a verb.

Examples: ܡܢ ܕܐܝܬ ܠܗ ܟܠܬܐ ܚܬܢܐ ܗܘ. He who has a bride is a groom.

131

The Dalath ܕ before the verb ܐܝܬ ܠܗ represents a relative pronoun following the interrogative He who ܡܢ . This rule applies to all interrogative pronouns. A more detailed explanation is forthcoming in future chapters in the study of verb.

A. Translate the following phrases into English and underscore the demonstrative pronoun in each sentences.

ܐ. ܗܢܐ ܓܒܪܐ ܕܐܝܬܘܗܝ ܟܬܒܐ.
_____

ܒ. ܗܕܐ ܛܠܝܬܐ.
_____

ܗ. ܗܠܝܢ ܓܒܪܐ ܘܗܠܝܢ ܢܫܐ.
_____

ܕ. ܗܘ ܓܒܪܐ ܘܗܝ ܐܢܬܬܐ.
_____

ܗ. ܗܘ ܓܒܪܐ ܗܘ ܛܠܝܬܐ.
_____

ܘ. ܗܢܘܢ ܗܘܝܬܝܢ ܗܠܝܢ ܗܘܝܬܢ.
_____

ܙ. ܗܢܘܢ ܗܘܝܬܝܢ ܗܠܝܢ ܗܘܝܬܢ.
_____

B. Translate the following sentences into Aramaic and underscore the Aramaic demonstrative pronouns.

1- This is a holy book.

2- This good queen.

3- These good girls; these good trees.

4- That bad boy and that bad girl.

5- Who is that boy? (distant)

6- Who is that queen? (distant)

7- These fruits and these mares. (near)

8- Those fruits and those mares. (distant)

REVIEW

1) Translate the following sentences into Aramaic.

1- These white books.

2- This good man.

3- The humble wife.

4- These good fruits.

5- These men of peace.

6- Those beautiful black horses.

7- What is his good name?

8- Who is he?

9- How many apostles of Jesus?

10- Which house?

11- What is this?

12- Who wrote this book?

13- Which high mountains?

14- That boy, that father, that mother.

____

15- Behold, the Lamb of God!

____

2) Translate the following sentences into English.

ܐ. ܡܵܢܵܘ ܫܡܵܟ݂.

ܐ. ____________________________________

ܒ. ܡܲܢܘܼ ܗܵܢܵܐ ܡܲܠܟܵܐ.

ܒ. ____________________________________

ܓ. ܐܲܝܢܘܼ ܒܲܝܬܲܟ݂ܘܿܢ.

ܓ. ____________________________________

ܕ. ܟܬ݂ܵܒ݂ܵܐ ܗܵܢܵܐ ܐܝܼܬ݂ܵܘܗܝ ܐܘܼܟ݂ܵܡܵܐ.

ܕ. ____________________________________

ܗ. ܗܵܠܹܝܢ ܢܶܫ̈ܶܐ ܢܲܟ݂ܦ̈ܵܬ݂ܵܐ.

ܗ. ____________________________________

ܘ. ܗܵܠܹܝܢ ܟܘܼܟ݂ܒܹ̈ܐ ܢܲܗܝܼܪܹ̈ܐ.

ܘ. ____________________________________

ܙ. ܗܵܢܘܿܢ ܟܬ݂ܵܒ݂ܹ̈ܐ ܚܕ̈ܲܬ݂ܹܐ.

ܛ. _____

ܝ. ܐܘܕܐ ܚܕܐ ܓܠܒܐ.

ܝ. _____

ܝܐ. ܐܢܐ ܗܘܝܬ ܗܘܝܢܐ ܦܘܠܘܣ.

ܝܐ. _____

ܝܒ. ܐܘܝ ܡܠܟܐ ܡܚܝܒܐ.

ܝܒ. _____

ܝܓ. ܐܘ ܙܒܢܐ ܕܐܬܐ ܕܗܕܐ ܕܣܒܪܐ.

ܝܓ. _____

ܝܕ. ܢܥܘܕ ܠܒܝܬܐ ܕܝܠܢ.

ܝܕ. _____

136

CHAPTER SEVEN

Verbs – An Introduction

CHAPTER SEVEN

UNIT ONE

VERBS: AN INTRODUCTION

Reading

ܐ. ܫܡܫܐ ܙܗܝܐ: ܝܗܒܐ ܚܝ̈ܐ ܢܘܗܪܐ ܘܚܡܝܡܘܬܐ ܘܚܝ̈ܐ.

ܒ. ܒܝܘܠܦܢܐ ܡܕܢܚ ܐܝܟܢܐ ܝܠܗ ܕܫܡܫܐ ܦܪܘܩ.

ܓ. ܡܠܟ̈ܐ ܣܓܕܘ ܠܐܠܗܐ ܕܒܫܡܝܐ.

ܕ. ܐܝܠܢ̈ܐ ܕܫܡܫܐ ܐܝܬܘܗܝ ܒܘܪܟܬܐ ܕܡܪܘܡܐ.

ܗ. ܬܫܒܘܚܬܐ ܠܐܠܗܐ ܒܡܪ̈ܘܡܐ.

ܘ. ܫܘܒܚܐ ܠܐܠܗܐ ܠܥܠܡ.

ܙ. ܪܘܚܐ ܕܩܘܕܫܐ ܐܝܬܘܗܝ ܠܘܬ ܟܠܢ .

ܚ. ܐܠܗܐ ܦܪܩ ܠܥܠܡܐ ܒܐܝܕܗ ܕܡܫܝܚܐ.

ܛ. ܡܠܟܘܬܐ ܕܫܡܝܐ ܩܪܝܒ ܠܢܦܫܟ.

ܝ. ܚܘܒܐ ܕܟܝܐ ܢܦܩ ܡܢ ܫܡܝܐ.

VOCABULARY

1- Way ܐܘܪܚܐ ܐܘܪܚܬܐ

2- There is / are ܐܝܬ

3- Blessing ܒܘܪܟܬܐ

4- Virgin, Virgins ܒܬܘܠܬܐ ܒܬܘܠܬܐ

5- Life ܚܝܐ

6- With, Toward ܥܡ

7- There is not / are none ܠܝܬ

8- Angel, Messenger ܡܠܐܟܐ

9- Highest, high region ܡܪܘܡܐ

10- Fell, will fall ܢܦܠ ܢܦܠ

11- Made, will make ܥܒܕ ܥܒܕ

12- Saved, will save ܦܪܩ ܢܦܪܘܩ

13- Cross ܨܠܝܒܐ

14- Killed, will kill ܩܛܠ ܢܩܛܘܠ

15- Holy Spirit ܪܘܚܐ ܕܩܘܕܫܐ

16- Praised, will praise ܫܒܚ. ܢܫܒܚ

17- Praise, glory ܫܘܒܚܐ

18- Heavens* ܫܡܝܐ

19- Truth ܫܪܪܐ

140

*NOTE: The Aramaic word ܫܡܝܐ may be translated in the singular – "heaven" or the plural – "heavens" The word also means "sky", "universe" and "cosmos".

1) **VERBS** - ܡܠܬܐ

A verb is a word that expresses action or a state of being (by itself) without the use of another word. (NOTE: The word Miltha - ܡܠܬܐ is feminine when it means "verb.") Aramaic verbs are formed by radical letters (root letters):

Bilateral (two radicals) stood - ܩܡ

Trilateral (three radicals) wrote - ܟܬܒ

Quadrilateral (four radicals) interpreted - ܦܫܩ

2) **USAGE OF VERBS**

   A. ACTIVE VOICE – He wrote   ܟܬܒ

   B. GENDER

      Masculine – He stands   ܩܐܡ

      Feminine – She stands   ܩܝܡܐ

   C. NUMBER

      Masculine Singular – He killed   ܩܛܠ

      Masculine Plural – They killed   ܩܛܠܘ

   D. PERSON – There are three persons.

      First Person – I write   ܟܬܒܢܐ

      Second Person – You write   ܟܬܒ ܐܢܬ

      Third Person – He writes   MOODS   ܟܬܒ

Indicative – He wrote ܟܬܒ

Imperative – write! ܟܬܘܒ

Infinitive – To write ܠܡܟܬܒ

E. TENSES There are three principal tenses.

Past ܘܗܢܐ ܕܟܬܒ - He wrote ܟܬܒ

Present ܘܗܢܐ ܕܟܬܒ - He writes ܟܬܒ

Future ܘܗܢܐ ܕܟܬܒ - He will write ܢܟܬܘܒ

NOTE: Some grammatical textbooks classify the tenses in the following manner:
Perfect tense – complete (past).
Imperfect tense – incomplete (future).

In the ancient Aramaic language the present tense may also indicate the future (Imperfect). It does not have a clear future tense as in the Greek and Latin languages.

The Defective Verbs:

1) ܐܝܬ   To be or to have.

2) ܠܝܬ   Not to be or not to have.

These two particular verbs are called defective because they do not follow the usual form for conjugating.

THE VERB – TO BE ܐܝܬ

Singular

First Person

M & F   – I am   ܐܢܐ ܐܝܬܝ

Second Person

M S   – You are   ܐܢܬ ܐܝܬܝܟ

F S   – You are   ܐܢܬܝ ܐܝܬܝܟܝ

Third Person

M S — He is   ܗܘ ܐܝܬܘܗܝ

F S — She is   ܗܝ ܐܝܬܝܗ̇

Plural

First Person

M & F — We are   ܚܢܢ ܐܝܬܝܢ

Second Person

M P — You are   ܐܢܬܘܢ ܐܝܬܝܟܘܢ

F P — You are   ܐܢܬܝܢ ܐܝܬܝܟܝܢ

Third Person

M P — They are   ܗܢܘܢ ܐܝܬܝܗܘܢ

F P — They are   ܗܢܝܢ ܐܝܬܝܗܝܢ

THE VERB – TO HAVE   ܐܝܬ ܠܗ

Singular

First Person

M & F — I have   ܐܝܬ ܠܝ

Second Person

M S — You have   ܐܝܬ ܠܟ

F S — You have   ܐܝܬ ܠܟܝ

Third Person

M S — He has ܐܝܬ ܠܗ

F S — She has ܐܝܬ ܠܗ̇

Plural

First Person

M & F — We have ܐܝܬ ܠܢ

Second Person

M P — You have ܐܝܬ ܠܟܘܢ

F P — You have ܐܝܬ ܠܟܝܢ

Third Person

M P — They have ܐܝܬ ܠܗܘܢ

F P — They have ܐܝܬ ܠܗܝܢ

THIRD VERB – NOT TO BE ܠܝܬ

Singular

First Person

M & F — I am not ܠܝܬܢ

Second Person

M S — You are not ܠܝܬܝܟ

F S — You are not ܠܝܬܝܟܝ

144

Third Person

M S	– He is not	ܠܹܐ ܝܗܘܿܘܹܗ
F S	– She is not	ܠܹܐ ܝܗܘܿܝܵܗ

Plural

First Person

M & F	– We are not	ܠܹܐ ܝܗܘܿܚ

Second Person

M P	– You are not	ܠܹܐ ܝܗܘܿܟ݂ܘܿܢ
F P	– You are not	ܠܹܐ ܝܗܘܿܟܹܝܢ

Third Person

M P	– They are not	ܠܹܐ ܝܗܘܿܢܘܿܢ
F P	– They are not	ܠܹܐ ܝܗܘܿܢܹܝܢ

THE VERB – NOT TO HAVE		ܠܹܐ ܝܬ

Singular

First Person

M & F	– I do not have	ܠܹܐ ܝܬܝ

Second Person

M S	– You do not have	ܠܹܐ ܝܬܟ݂
F S	– You do not have	ܠܹܐ ܝܬܟ݂ܝ

Third Person

M S	– He does not have	ܠܹܗ ܠܹܗ
F S	– She does not have	ܠܹܗ ܠܵܗ

Plural

First Person

M & F	– We do not have	ܠܹܗ ܠܲܢ

Second Person

M P	– You do not have	ܠܹܗ ܠܲܟ݂ܘܿܢ
F P	– You do not have	ܠܹܗ ܠܲܟ݂ܝܢ

Third Person

M P	– They do not have	ܠܹܗ ܠܗܘܿܢ
F P	– They do not have	ܠܹܗ ܠܗܝܢ

REVIEW

1- Conjugate the verbs "to be" and "not to be" three times each.

   A. To be   ܐܝܼܬ

_____ _____ _____
_____ _____ _____
_____ _____ _____
_____ _____ _____

B. Not to be ܠܹܐ ܗ݇ܘܹܐ

2- Write the verbs "to have" and "not to have" three times each.

A. To have ܐܝܼܬ ܠܹܗ

B. Not to have ܠܹܗ ܠܹܐ

3- Translate the following sentences into Aramaic.

1) I am a good man.

2) You are a bad disciple.

3) She is a beautiful woman.

4) He is a tall boy.

5) Those black mountains are high.

6) He is not a bad boy.

7) Thomas has a book.

8) Mary does not have the holy books.

9) The priest does not have a cross.

10) I am not a king; I am a human being.

4- Translate the following sentences into English.

ܐ. ܡܠܟܬܐ ܕܝܗ݇ܘ ܥܦܝܦܬܐ.

ܐ.

ܒ. ܩܕܝܫܐ ܐܝܬ ܠܗ ܨܠܝܒܐ ܕܘܗܒܐ ܡܕܝܢܬܐ.

ܒ.

ܗ. ܛܘܪܐ ܩܛܠܝܬܐ ܕܝܗ݇ܘܢ ܪܡܐ.

ܗ.

ܕ. ܠܝܬ ܠܝ ܟܬܒܐ.

ܕ.

ܗ. ܠܒܝܼܫܹܗ ܦܹܠܓܹܐ ܕܝܼܢܘܿ ܓܢܝܼܒܹ̈ܐ.

ܗ. _____ .

ܘ. ܦܹܠܓܹܐ ܠܒܼܗ ܠܗܘܢ ܚܘܿܒܹܐ ܒܙܕܝܼܢܹܐ.

ܘ. _____ .

ܙ. ܩܘܼܢܹܐ ܕܣܘܼܒܹܟܹ̈ܐ ܕܝܼܘܘܼܝܼ ܠܩܡ ܒܝܼܬ݂ܹ̈ܐ.

ܙ. _____ .

ܚ. ܒܘܼܒܒܼܘܢ ܒܢܝܼܬܹ̈ܐ ܕܝܼܘܡܢ ܫܝܼܬܹܐ.

ܚ. _____ .

ܛ. ܐܢܗܘܿ ܕܝܼܗܝܼܒܼܬ ܒܘܠܬܹܐ.

ܛ. _____ .

ܝ. ܐܢܗܘܢ ܕܝܼܒ ܠܓܘܢ ܠܩܡ ܘܒܬ݂ܪ.

ܝ. _____ .

UNIT TWO

Past Tense Indicative Mood (Perfect Tense)

The usual form of the verb before conjugation is always put in the third person masculine singular.

Example – He wrote ܟ݁ܬ݂ܰܒ݂ (Past Tense)

He killed ܩܛܰܠ (Past Tense) or He saved ܦ݁ܪܰܩ (Past Tense)

The conjugation of the verbs in the Past Tense, Active Voice.

THE VERB – TO WRITE ܟ݁ܬ݂ܰܒ݂

Singular

First Person

M & F   - I wrote   (ܶܬ݂)   ܟ݁ܶܬ݂ܒ݁ܶܬ݂

Second Person

M S   - You wrote   (ܬ݁)   ܟ݁ܬ݂ܰܒ݂ܬ݁

F S   - You wrote   (ܬ݁ܝ)   ܟ݁ܬ݂ܰܒ݂ܬ݁ܝ

Third Person

M S   - He wrote   (—)   ܟ݁ܬ݂ܰܒ݂

F S   - She wrote   (ܰܬ݂)   ܟ݁ܶܬ݂ܒ݁ܰܬ݂

Plural

First Person

M & F   - We wrote   (ܢ) or (ܢܰܢ)   ܟ݁ܬ݂ܰܒ݂ܢ or ܟ݁ܬ݂ܰܒ݂ܢܰܢ

Second Person

M P - You wrote   (ܟܘܢ)   ܟܬܒܟܘܢ

F P - You wrote   (ܟܝܢ)   ܟܬܒܟܝܢ

Third Person

M P - They wrote   (ܘܢ) or (ܘ)   ܟܬܒܘܢ or ܟܬܒܘ

F P - They wrote   (ܝܢ) or (ܢ)   ܟܬܒܝܢ or ܟܬܒܢ

THE VERB - TO SAVE   ܦܪܩ

Singular

First Person

M & F   - I saved   (ܶܩܠܝ)   ܦܪܩܠܝ

Second Person:

M S - You saved   (ܬ)   ܦܪܩܬ

F S - You saved   (ܬܝ)   ܦܪܩܬܝ

Third Person:

M S - He saved   (—)   ܦܪܩ

F S - She saved   (ܬ)   ܦܪܩܬ

Plural

First Person

M & F - We saved   (ܢ) or (ܢܢ)   ܦܪܩܢ or ܦܪܩܢܢ

152

Second Person

M P   - You saved   (ܬܘܢ)   ܩܕܡܬܘܢ

F P   - You saved   (ܬܝܢ)   ܩܕܡܬܝܢ

Third Person

M P   - They saved   (ܘ) or (ܘܢ)   ܩܕܡܘ   or   ܩܕܡܘܢ

F P   - They saved   (ܹܝܢ) or (‒)   ܩܕܡܝܢ   or   ܩܕܡ

NOTE: In the second person feminine plural singular – taw Yodh ܬܝ , the Yodh ܝ is written but it is not pronounced. The same rule applies to the third person masculine plural. The Waw ܘ is written but it is not pronounced. Also, the Siyame ̈ must be added in all verbs in the third person feminine plural only.

The Defective Verbs - ܐܝܬ and ܗܘܐ in the past tense.

THE VERB – TO BE ܐܝܬ PAST TENSE – WAS.

Singular

First Person

M & F   – I was   ܐܝܬ ܗܘܝܬ

Second Person

M S   – You were   ܐܝܬ ܗܘܝܬ

F S   – You were   ܐܝܬ ܗܘܝܬܝ

Third Person

M S	– He was	ܐܝܼܬܼܘܗܝ ܗܘܵܐ
F S	– She was	ܐܝܼܬܼܝܗ ܗܘܵܗ

Plural

First Person

M & F	– We were	ܐܝܼܬܼܝܢ ܗܘܵܝܢ

Second Person

M P	– You were	ܐܝܼܬܼܟܼܘܢ ܗܘܵܘܟܼܘܢ
F P	– You were	ܐܝܼܬܼܟܼܝܢ ܗܘܵܝܬܹܝܢ

Third Person

M P	– They were	ܐܝܼܬܼܝܗܘܢ ܗܘܵܘ
F P	– They were	ܐܝܼܬܼܝܗܝܢ ܗܘܵܝ

THE VERB – NOT TO BE ܠܝܬ **PAST TENSE – WAS NOT.**

Singular

First Person

M & F	- I was not	ܠܝܬܼܝ ܗܘܵܐ

Second Person

M S	- You were not	ܠܝܬܼܝܟ ܗܘܵܐ
F S	- You were not	ܠܝܬܼܟܝ ܗܘܵܝ

Third Person

M S   - He was not   ܠܝܬܘܗܝ ܗܘܐ

F S   - She was not   ܠܝܬܝܗ ܗܘܬ

Plural

First Person

M & F   - We were not   ܠܝܬܝܢ ܗܘܝܢ

Second Person

M P   - You were not   ܠܝܬܝܟܘܢ ܗܘܝܬܘܢ

F P   - You were not   ܠܝܬܝܟܝܢ ܗܘܝܬܝܢ

Third Person

M P   - They were not   ܠܝܬܝܗܘܢ ܗܘܘ

F P   - They were not   ܠܝܬܝܗܝܢ ܗܘܝ

THE VERB – TO HAVE   ܐܝܬ ܠܝ   PAST TENSE – HAD

Singular

First Person

M & F   - I had   ܐܝܬ ܗܘܐ ܠܝ

Second Person

M S   - You had   ܐܝܬ ܗܘܐ ܠܟ

F S   - You had   ܐܝܬ ܗܘܐ ܠܟܝ

Third Person

M S   - He had   ܐܝܬ ܗܘܵܐ ܠܹܗ

F S   - She had   ܐܝܬ ܗܘܵܐ ܠܵܗ̇

Plural

First Person

M & F   - We had   ܐܝܬ ܗܘܵܐ ܠܲܢ

Second Person

M P   - You had   ܐܝܬ ܗܘܵܐ ܠܵܟ݂ܘܿܢ

F P   - You had   ܐܝܬ ܗܘܵܐ ܠܵܟ݂ܶܝܢ

Third Person

M P   - They had   ܐܝܬ ܗܘܵܐ ܠܗܘܿܢ

F P   - They had   ܐܝܬ ܗܘܵܐ ܠܗܶܝܢ

THE VERB – NOT TO HAVE ܠܲܝܬ - PAST TENSE – DID NOT HAVE

Singular

First Person

M & F   - I didn't have   ܠܲܝܬ ܗܘܵܐ ܠܝܼ

Second Person

M S   - You didn't have   ܠܲܝܬ ܗܘܵܐ ܠܵܟ݂

F S   - You didn't have   ܠܲܝܬ ܗܘܵܐ ܠܵܟ݂ܝ

Third Person

M S   - He didn't have   ܠܹܗ ܗܘܵܐ ܠܹܗ

F S   - She didn't have   ܠܹܗ ܗܘܵܐ ܠܵܗ

Plural

First Person

M & F - We didn't have   ܠܹܗ ܗܘܵܐ ܠܲܢ

Second Person

M P   - You didn't have   ܠܹܗ ܗܘܵܐ ܠܵܟ݂ܘܿܢ

F P   - You didn't have   ܠܹܗ ܗܘܵܐ ܠܵܟ݂ܹܝܢ

Third Person

M P   - They didn't have   ܠܹܗ ܗܘܵܐ ܠܗܘܿܢ

F P   - They didn't have   ܠܹܗ ܗܘܵܐ ܠܗܹܝܢ

REVIEW

1- Conjugate the following verbs in the past tense.

ܚܙܹܐ   ܦܬܚ   ܢܦܲܩ

_____   _____   _____

_____   _____   _____

_____   _____   _____

_____   _____   _____

2- Translate the following sentences into Aramaic.

1) The apostles wrote the holy books.

2) The disciples of Jesus were good men.

3) Thomas is an apostle of truth.

4) Those good men were men of God.

5) Our women were beautiful and are beautiful this day.

6) The bear killed those red mares.

7) God's angels are in heaven and on earth.

8) The cross of Jesus is a blessing.

9) Jesus's mother's name is Mary.

---

10) Jesus said, "I am the way, the truth and the life ".

---

11) We have five holy books at home.

---

12) I had the holy books in the temple.

---

13) John wasn't in the house. I was in the house.

---

14) He said the words and they wrote the words in that large book.

3- Translate the following sentences into English.

ܐ. ܫܘܒܚܐ ܠܐܒܐ ܘܠܒܪܐ ܘܠܪܘܚܐ ܕܩܘܕܫܐ.

ܐ. ______________________________

ܒ. ܐܠܗܐ ܐܝܬܘܗܝ ܚܘܒܐ.

ܒ. ______________________________

ܓ. ܡܠܐܟܐ ܕܡܪܝܐ ܐܬܐ ܠܒܝܬܐ ܕܡܪܝܡ ܘܐܡܪ ܠܗ̇: ܫܠܡ ܠܟܝ ܡܪܝܡ

ܓ. ______________________________

ܕ. ܝܫܘܥ ܐܝܬܘܗܝ ܒܪܗ ܕܐܠܗܐ.

ܕ. ______________________________

UNIT THREE

PRESENT TENSE INDICATIVE MOOD

There are many rules for forming the present tense. For beginners the following rules are sufficient.

A. Bilateral verbs are formed in the following manner:

To stand (stood) ܩܵܡ the letter Alap ܐ is added as a medial letter.

- ܩܵܐܡ = ܡ + ܐ + ܩ Standing (present tense or present participle).

B. Trilateral verbs are formed in the following manner:

A Zqapa ܵ is added on the first radical and a Pthaha ܲ or a Zlama qashya ܹ may be added on the second radical.

To open (opened) ܦܬܲܚ opens or is opening ܦܵܬܲܚ

To kill (killed) ܩܛܸܠ kills or is killing ܩܵܛܸܠ

C. Quadrilateral verbs are formed in the following manner:

Non – vocalized Meem ܡ is prefixed to the past tense of the verb.

To disciple (disciple) ܬܲܠܡܸܕ disciples or is discipline ܡܬܲܠܡܸܕ

D. When conjugating the present tense, subject pronouns (personal pronouns) are used and in some cases they are suffixed to the verb.

REMINDER: The present tense indicates the following:

1) I write
2) I do write
3) I am writing

THE VERB – TO WRITE ܟܵܬܹܒ

Singular

First Person

M S	- I write	ܟܵܬܹܒ ܐܵܢܵܐ
F S	- I write	ܟܵܬܒܵܐ ܐܵܢܵܐ

Second Person

M S	- You write	ܟܵܬܹܒ ܝܘܹܬ
F S	- You write	ܟܵܬܒܵܐ ܝܘܵܬܝ

Third Person

M S	- He writes	ܟܵܬܹܒ
F S	- She writes	ܟܵܬܒܵܐ

Plural

First Person

M S	- We write	ܟܵܬܒܝܼܢ
F S	- We write	ܟܵܬܒܵܢ

Second Person

M S	- You write	ܟܵܬܒܝܼܬܘܿܢ
F S	- You write	ܟܵܬܒܵܬܹܢ

Third Person

M S	- They write	ܟܵܬܒܝܼ
F S	- They write	ܟܵܬܒܵܢ

NOTE: The present tense takes a large point over the middle letter of the verb when conjugating.

Example ܢܵܥܹܡ (See Ch. 2, p. 78, rule A- "In Verbs.")

REVIEW

1- Conjugate the following verbs in the present tense.

ܢܵܓܹܒ	ܢܵܥܹܡ	ܢܵܓܹܕ
_____	_____	_____
_____	_____	_____
_____	_____	_____
_____	_____	_____
_____	_____	_____
_____	_____	_____
_____	_____	_____
_____	_____	_____
_____	_____	_____
_____	_____	_____

2- Translate the following sentences into English.

ܐ. ܣܘܣܝ̈ܐ ܐܘܟܡ̈ܐ ܐܙܠܝܢ ܠܒܬ̈ܝܗܘܢ.

ܐ. ____

ܒ. ܥܠܝܡ̈ܐ ܐܙܠܝܢ ܥܡ ܝܥܩܘܒ.

ܒ. ____

ܓ. ܟܗ̈ܢܐ ܡܨܠܝܢ ܒܗܝܟܠܐ.

ܓ. ____

ܕ. ܢܫ̈ܐ ܡܫܒܚܢ ܠܐܠܗܐ.

ܕ. ____

ܗ. ܒܢ̈ܝܗܘܢ ܩܪܝܢ ܐܡܗܘܢ ܘܐܒܘܗܘܢ .

ܗ. ____

ܘ. ܝܥܩܘܒ ܩܪܐ ܠܬܠܡܝ̈ܕܐ ܡܢ ܚܝܒܘܬܐ.

ܘ. ____

ܙ. ܛܠܝܐ ܪܟܒ ܥܠ ܣܘܣܐ.

ܙ. ____

ܚ. ܒܢ̈ܬܐ ܫܩ̈ܠܢ ܣܦܪ̈ܐ.

ܚ. ____

ܛ. ܡܠܦ̈ܢܐ ܐܡܪ: ܐܢܬܘܢ ܐܝܬܘܢ ܬܠܡܝ̈ܕܐ ܛܒ̈ܐ.

_____ .ܠ

ܢ .. ܠܝܕ ܡܢܚܢܣ ܠܡܢܕܢܐ.

_____ .ܢ

UNIT FOUR

The Future Tense Indicative Mood (Imperfect Tense)

There are many rules for forming the future tense. For beginners the following rules are sufficient.

A- Bilateral verbs that carry a Zqapa ◌ܳ become Rwasa ܘ

Example: to stand (stood) ܩܳܡ, I will stand ܐܩܘܡ

NOTE: (Alap ܐ is used for the first person singular) but, when the verb carries a Pthaha ◌ܰ some bilateral verbs remain the same and others become Rwaha ܿܘ

Examples: Desired ܨܒܰܐ , I will desire ܐܨܒܰܐ (NOTE: The Pthaha did not change).

Plundered ܒܰܙ , I will plunder ܐܒܘܙ (NOTE: The Pthaha becomes a Rwaha).

B- Trilateral verbs may become a Rwaha ܿܘ or remain the same.

Example: was jealous ܚܣܰܡ, I will be jealous ܐܚܣܰܡ (NOTE: There is no change in the verb "jealous").

Killed ܩܛܰܠ , I will kill ܐܩܛܘܠ (NOTE: The Pthaha becomes a Rwaha).

C- Quadrilateral verbs make no changes in their root.

D- Example: Interpreted ܦܰܫܶܩ , I will interpret ܐܦܰܫܶܩ

165

THE VERB - TO SAVE ܦܵܪܹܩ

Singular

First Person

M & F — I will save   ܒܹܦܵܪܹܩ

Second Person

M S — You will save   ܒܸܬ ܦܵܪܹܩ

F S — You will save   ܒܸܬ ܦܵܪܩܝ

Third Person

M S — He will save   ܒܝܦܵܪܹܩ

F S — She will save   ܒܸܬ ܦܵܪܹܩ

Plural

First Person

M & F — We will save   ܒܝܦܵܪܹܩ

Second Person

M P — You will save   ܒܸܬ ܦܵܪܩܘܢ

F P — You will save   ܒܸܬ ܦܵܪܩܢ

Third Person

M P — They will save   ܒܝܦܵܪܩܘܢ

F P — They will save   ܒܝܦܵܪܩܢ

The Defective Verbs - ܐܬܹܐ and ܝܵܗܒ in the future tense.

THE VERB – TO BE ܐܝܬ FUTURE TENSE – WILL BE.

Singular

First Person

M & F — I will be ܐܗܘܢ ܐܝܼܬܼܝ

Second Person

M S — You will be ܗܘܢ ܐܝܼܬܼܝܟ

F S — You will be ܗܘܝ ܐܝܼܬܼܝܟܝ

Third Person

M S — He will be ܢܗܘܐ ܐܝܼܬܼܘܗܝ

F S — She will be ܗܘܐ ܐܝܼܬܼܝܗ

Plural

First Person

M & F — We will be ܢܗܘܐ ܐܝܼܬܼܢ

Second Person

M P — You will be ܗܘܘܢ ܐܝܼܬܼܟܘܢ

F P — You will be ܗܘܝܢ ܐܝܼܬܼܟܝܢ

Third Person

M P — They will be ܢܗܘܘܢ ܐܝܼܬܼܝܗܘܢ

F P — They will be ܢܗܘܝܢ ܐܝܼܬܼܝܗܝܢ

THE VERB - NOT TO BE ܠܹܐ ܗܵܘܹܐ FUTURE TENSE – WILL NOT BE

Singular

First Person

M & F   - I will not be   ܒܹܬ ܠܹܐ ܗܵܘܹܢ

Second Person

M S   - You will not be   ܒܹܬ ܠܹܐ ܗܵܘܹܬ

F S   - You will not be   ܒܹܬ ܠܹܐ ܗܵܘܝܵܬܝ

Third Person

M S   - He will not be   ܒܹܬ ܠܹܐ ܗܵܘܹܐ

F S   - She will not be   ܒܹܬ ܠܹܐ ܗܵܘܝܵܐ

Plural

First Person

M & F   - We will not be   ܒܹܬ ܠܹܐ ܗܵܘܲܚ

Second Person

M P   - You will not be   ܒܹܬ ܠܹܐ ܗܵܘܝܼܬܘܿܢ

F P   - You will not be   ܒܹܬ ܠܹܐ ܗܵܘܝܵܬܹܝܢ

Third Person

M P   - They will not be   ܒܹܬ ܠܹܐ ܗܵܘܝܼܘܿܢ

F P   - They will not be   ܒܹܬ ܠܹܐ ܗܵܘܝܵܢ

THE VERB – TO HAVE ܐܝܬ ܠܗ FUTURE TENSE – WILL HAVE

Singular

First Person

M & F   - I will have   ܐܗܘܐ ܐܝܬ ܠܝ

Second Person

M S   - You will have   ܐܗܘܐ ܐܝܬ ܠܘܟ

F S   - You will have   ܐܗܘܐ ܐܝܬ ܠܟܝ

Third Person

M S   - He will have   ܐܗܘܐ ܐܝܬ ܠܗ

F S   - She will have   ܐܗܘܐ ܐܝܬ ܠܗ̇

Plural

First Person

M & F   - We will have   ܐܗܘܐ ܐܝܬ ܠܢ

Second Person

M P   - You will have   ܐܗܘܐ ܐܝܬ ܠܟܘܢ

F P   - You will have   ܐܗܘܐ ܐܝܬ ܠܟܝܢ

Third Person

M P   - They will have   ܐܗܘܐ ܐܝܬ ܠܗܘܢ

F P   - They will have   ܐܗܘܐ ܐܝܬ ܠܗܝܢ

THE VERB – NOT TO HAVE ܠܝܬ ܠܗ   FUTURE TENSE – WILL NOT HAVE

Singular

First Person

| M & F | - I will not have | ܒܕ ܠܝܬ ܗܘܝ |

Second Person

| M S | - You will not have | ܠܟ ܠܝܬ ܗܘܝܬ |
| F S | - You will not have | ܠܟܝ ܠܝܬ ܗܘܝ |

Third Person

| M S | - He will not have | ܠܗ ܠܝܬ ܗܘܝ |
| F S | - She will not have | ܠܗܿ ܠܝܬ ܗܘܝ |

Plural

First Person

| M & F | - We will not have | ܠܢ ܠܝܬ ܗܘܝ |

Second Person

| M P | - You will not have | ܠܟܘܢ ܠܝܬ ܗܘܝ |
| F P | - You will not have | ܠܟܝܢ ܠܝܬ ܗܘܝ |

Third Person

| M P | - They will not have | ܠܗܘܢ ܠܝܬ ܗܘܝ |
| F P | - They will not have | ܠܗܝܢ ܠܝܬ ܗܘܝ |

REVIEW

1- Conjugate the following verbs in the future tense.

ܐܶܟܬܽܘܒ	ܐܶܙܪܽܘܥ	ܐܶܦܪܽܘܩ
I will write	I will plant	I will save.

2- Translate the following sentences into Aramaic.

1) The snow will fall on the house.

2) The men will praise God in his holy temple.

3) The bear will kill the man.

4) The good men will write in the holy books.

5) The apostle Thomas will build the house of God.

6) You (F P) will plunder the house of the evil man.

7) The bull will kill the horse.

8) The Holy Spirit will save friends of the apostles.

9) The hand of the lord God will fall on the people.

10) The mother will save her daughter from the evil image.

3- Translate the following sentences into English.

ܐ. ܢܟܬܘܒ ܒܝܬܐ ܠܚܒܪܐ .

ܐ. _____

ܒ. ܩܛܠܢܐ ܝܘܕܐ ܒܝܫܐ .

ܒ. _____

ܓ. ܐܒܗܬ̈ܢ ܗܘܘ ܓܒܪ̈ܐ ܛܒ̈ܐ.

ܓ. _____

ܕ. ܝܕܐ ܕܐܢܫܐ ܡܢ ܐܠܗܘܬܐ.

ܒ. ‎_____

ܗ. ܥܠܒܝܢܐ ܗܕܐ ܗܘܘܗܐ ܕܓܘܕܓܕ ܠܥܝܠܥܝܢ ܕܢܠܟܢܐ.

ܗ. ‎_____

ܘ. ܒܥܘܕ ܣܘܘܕ ܚܢܘܘܐ ܗܠܝܢܝܐ.

ܘ. ‎_____

ܙ. ܘܩܕܡܐ ܝܗܒ ܠܗܢܝܐ ܠܢܘܣܦܘܗܝ.

ܙ. ‎_____

ܚ. ܩܠܟܐ ܘܩܕܡܐ ܘܥܕܡܐ ܠܟ ܥܕܢܐ.

ܚ. ‎_____

ܛ. ܩܕܡܐ ܝܗܒܢܢ ܡܢ ܚܛܐ.

ܛ. ‎_____

ܝ. ܢܠܟܢܐ ܕܓܗܘܒ ܥܩܗܘܬ ܕܥܡܝܢܐ.

ܝ. ‎_____

THE LORD'S PRAYER in Classical Aramaic

Matthew 6:9 – 13

ܐܒܘܢ ܕܒܫܡܝܐ. ܢܬܩܕܫ ܫܡܟ.

ܬܐܬܐ ܡܠܟܘܬܟ. ܢܗܘܐ ܨܒܝܢܟ. ܐܝܟܢܐ ܕܒܫܡܝܐ ܐܦ ܒܐܪܥܐ.

173

ܘܗܒ ܠܢ ܠܚܡܐ ܕܣܘܢܩܢܢ ܝܘܡܢܐ.

ܘܫܒܘܩ ܠܢ ܚܘܒܝܢ. ܐܝܟܢܐ ܕܐܦ ܚܢܢ ܫܒܩܢ ܠܚܝܒܝܢ.

ܘܠܐ ܬܥܠܢ ܠܢܣܝܘܢܐ. ܐܠܐ ܦܨܢ ܡܢ ܒܝܫܐ. ܡܛܠ ܕܕܝܠܟ ܗܝ ܡܠܟܘܬܐ.

ܘܚܝܠܐ ܘܬܫܒܘܚܬܐ. ܠܥܠܡ ܥܠܡܝܢ.

ܐܡܝܢ ܀

THE BEATITUDES

Matthew 5:3 – 9

ܓ: ܛܘܒܝܗܘܢ ܠܡܣܟܢܐ ܒܪܘܚ. ܕܕܝܠܗܘܢ ܗܝ ܡܠܟܘܬܐ ܕܫܡܝܐ.

ܕ: ܛܘܒܝܗܘܢ ܠܐܒܝܠܐ. ܕܗܢܘܢ ܢܬܒܝܐܘܢ.

ܗ: ܛܘܒܝܗܘܢ ܠܡܟܝܟܐ. ܕܗܢܘܢ ܢܐܪܬܘܢ ܐܪܥܐ.

ܘ: ܛܘܒܝܗܘܢ ܠܐܝܠܝܢ ܕܟܦܢܝܢ ܘܨܗܝܢ ܠܟܐܢܘܬܐ. ܕܗܢܘܢ ܢܣܒܥܘܢ.

ܙ: ܛܘܒܝܗܘܢ ܠܡܪܚܡܢܐ. ܕܥܠܝܗܘܢ ܢܗܘܘܢ ܪܚܡܐ.

ܚ: ܛܘܒܝܗܘܢ ܠܐܝܠܝܢ ܕܕܟܝܢ ܒܠܒܗܘܢ. ܕܗܢܘܢ ܢܚܙܘܢ ܠܐܠܗܐ.

ܛ: ܛܘܒܝܗܘܢ ܠܥܒܕܝ ܫܠܡܐ. ܕܒܢܘܗܝ ܕܐܠܗܐ ܢܬܩܪܘܢ.

NOTE: The vocabulary for the Lord's Prayer and the Beatitudes will be found in the Aramaic – English dictionary beginning on P.175.

DICTIONARY
ARAMAIC – ENGLISH

A	ܐ
August	ܐܒ
Abbot	ܐܒܐ
Father, Fathers	ܐܒܐ ܐܒܗܐ
Lost	ܐܒܕ ܐܒܝܕ
Mourner	ܐܒܝܠܐ
Reward	ܐܓܪܐ
Adam	ܐܕܡ
Ear	ܐܕܢܐ
Black	ܐܘܟܡܐ
Way	ܐܘܪܚܐ
Went	ܐܙܠ
Brother	ܐܚܐ
Hand	ܐܝܕܐ
Even as	ܐܝܟܢܐ
Tree	ܐܝܠܢܐ
Day	ܐܝܡܡܐ

There is \ are (to be)	ܐܝܬ
Eat	ܐܲܟ݂ܸܠ: ܐܵܟܹܘܿܠ
But	ܐܲܠܵܐ
God	ܐܲܠܵܗܵܐ
Mother	ܐܸܡܵܐ ܐܸܡܵܬ݂ܵܐ
Said	ܐܸܡܹܪ ܒܹܐܡܵܪܵܐ
Lamb	ܐܸܡܪܵܐ
Man / Anyone / Person	ܐܢܵܫܵܐ
Woman / Wife / Women	ܐܲܢ݇ܬ݁ܬ݂ܵܐ (ܒܲܟ݂ܬܵܐ)
Also	ܐܵܦ
Rabbit	ܐܲܪܢܒ݂ܵܐ
Earth	ܐܲܪܥܵܐ

B

To Bubble	ܒܲܒܹܒ݂
Baghdad	ܒܲܓ݂ܕܲܕ
Foolish	ܒܗܵܐ
Prosperity	ܒܘܼܣܵܡܵܐ
Blessing	ܒܘܼܪܟ݁ܬ݂ܵܐ
Consoled	ܒܘܼܝܵܐܵܐ

Canal	ܒܝܼܢܵܐ
Bad / Evil	ܒܝܼܫܵܐ
House / Houses	ܒܲܝܬܵܐ : ܒܵܬܹܐ
Built	ܒܢܵܐ : ܒܵܢܹܐ
Nice, sweet, delicious	ܒܣܝܼܡܵܐ
Mosquito	ܒܩܵܐ
Son, Sons	ܒܪܵܐ : ܒܢܘܿܢܹܐ
Created	ܒܪܹܐ : ܒܪܵܐ ܒܵܪܹܐ
Blest	ܒܪܝܼܟ
Man / Human being	ܒܲܪܢܵܫܵܐ
Daughter / Daughters	(ܒܪܲܬ) ܒܪܵܬܵܐ ܒܢܵܬܹܐ
Virgin / Virgins	ܒܬܘܿܠܬܵܐ ܒܬܘܿܠܵܬܹܐ
G	**ܓ**
Side	ܓܒܵܐ
Man / Husband	ܓܲܒܪܵܐ
Fortune	ܓܲܕܵܐ
Time	ܓܵܗܵܐ
Inside	ܓܵܘܵܐ
Den / Well	ܓܘܼܒܵܐ

Wall	ܟܘܬܠܐ
Treasure	ܟܢܙܐ
Thief	ܓܢܒܐ
Camel	ܓܡܠܐ
Cave	ܟܐܦܐ
Bone	ܓܪܡܐ
D	ܕ
Wolf	ܕܐܒܐ
Bear	ܕܒܐ
Place	ܕܘܟܐ
Pure	ܕܟܝܐ
Judgment	ܕܝܢܐ
Blood	ܕܡܐ
H	ܗ
Behold	ܗܐ
Temple	ܗܝܟܠܐ
Walked	ܗܠܟ ܗܠܟ

W	ܘ
Rose / Flower	ܘܲܪܕܵܐ
Z	ܙ
Bell	ܙܲܓܵܐ
Righteous	ܙܲܕܝܼܩܵܐ
Small	ܙܥܘܿܪܵܐ
H	ܚ
Beloved	ܚܲܒܝܼܒ
Destroyed	ܚܒܝܼܠ ܚܫܝܼܠ
To make joyful	ܚܲܕܝܼ
Love	ܚܘܼܒܵܐ
Debt / Offense	ܚܘܿܒܵܐ
White	ܚܸܘܵܪܵܐ
Saw	ܚܙܵܐ ܝܼܣܘܿܥ
Sin	ܚܛܝܼܬ݂ܵܐ
Alive / Living	ܚܲܝܵܐ ܚܲܝܹܐ
Life	ܚܲܝܹܐ
Jaw	ܚܲܢܟܵܐ
Wise	ܚܲܟܝܼܡܵܐ

179

Wisdom	ܣܘܟܠܐ
Milk	ܚܠܒܐ
Wedding	ܚܠܘܠܐ
Dream	ܚܠܡܐ
Merciful	ܚܢܢܐ
Pagan	ܚܢܦܐ
Harvest	ܚܨܕܐ
Spear	ܢܝܙܟܐ

T

ܛ

Good	ܛܒܐ
Cook	ܛܒܚܐ
Happy / Delighted. Blessed	ܛܘܒܢܐ
Mountain	ܛܘܪܐ
Grace	ܛܝܒܘܬܐ
Boy / Boys	ܛܠܝܐ : ܛܠܝܐ̈
Girl / Girls	ܛܠܝܬܐ : ܛܠܝܬܐ̈

Y

ܝ

John	ܝܘܚܢܢ
Day	ܝܘܡܐ

Jonah	ܝܘܢܢ
Joseph	ܝܘܣܦ
Sea	ܝܡܐ
Inherit	ܝܪܬ ܝܪܬܐ
Jesus	ܝܫܘܥ

K

Pious / Just / Kind	ܟܐܢܐ
Justice / Goodness	ܟܐܢܘܬܐ
Stone / Rock	ܟܐܦܐ
Simon Peter	ܫܡܥܘܢ ܟܐܦܐ
Priest	ܟܗܢܐ
Thorn	ܟܘܒܐ
Star	ܟܘܟܒܐ
All	ܟܠ
Laughed	ܟܣܝ
Dog	ܟܠܒܐ
Bride	ܟܠܬܐ
December	ܟܢܘܢ

181

January	ܟܢܘܢ ܒ
To Hunger	ܟܦܢ ܢܟܦܢ
Wrote	ܟܬܒ
Book	ܟܬܒܐ
Linen Cloth	ܟܬܢܐ
L	ܠ
No	ܠܐ
Heart	ܠܒܐ
To / With Toward	ܠܘܬ
Bread	ܠܚܡܐ
There is none / Are none	ܠܝܬ
Night	ܠܠܝܐ
Forever	ܠܥܠܡ
M	ܡ
Meek / Humble	ܡܟܝܟܐ
Angel	ܡܠܐܟܐ
Salt	ܡܠܚܐ
King	ܡܠܟܐ
Queen / Queens	ܡܠܟܬܐ : ܡܠܟܬܐ

Teacher	ܡܠܦܢܐ
Word / Words	ܡܠܬܐ : ܡܠܐ
From	ܡܢ
What	ܡܢܐ
Poor	ܡܣܟܢܐ
Sir / Lord	ܡܪܐ
Highest / High region	ܡܪܘܡܐ
Bold	ܡܪܚܐ
Lord God	ܡܪܝܐ ܐܠܗܐ
Mary / Miriam	ܡܪܝܡ
Mark	ܡܪܩܘܣ
Christ / Messiah	ܡܫܝܚܐ
Skin	ܡܫܟܐ
Drink	ܡܫܬܝܐ

N

Let there be / Will be	ܢܗܘܐ : ܢܗܘܘܢ
Fish	ܢܘܢܐ
Fire	ܢܘܪܐ
Rest	ܢܝܚܐ

Temptation	ܢܣܝܘܢܐ
Fell	ܢܦܠ : ܢܦܝܠ

S

To Satisfy	ܣܒܥ — ܣܒܵܥܐ
Martyr	ܣܗܕܐ
Moon	ܣܗܪܐ
Red	ܣܘܡܩܐ
Need	ܣܘܢܩܢܐ
Horse / Mare	ܣܘܣܝܐ : ܣܘܣܬܐ
Track	ܣܚܪܐ
Blind	ܣܡܝܐ
Wart	ܣܛܐ

A

Feast	ܥܐܕܐ
Did / Made / Work	ܥܒܕ ܥܒܝܕ
Chest	ܥܘܒܐ
Eye	ܥܝܢܐ
On / Upon / Over / Above	ܥܠ

To Enter	ܥܲܒ݂ܸܕ : ܝܼܥܡܸܕ
World	ܥܲܠܡܵܐ
Gust / Hurricane	ܥܲܠܥܵܠܵܐ
With	ܥܲܡ
People	ܥܲܡܵܐ
Friday	ܥܪܘܼܒ݂ܬܵܐ
P	ܦ
Fruit	ܦܹܐܪܵܐ
Mouth	ܦܘܼܡܵܐ
Nose	ܦܘܼܩܵܐ
Elephant	ܦܝܼܠܵܐ
Pope	ܦܵܦܵܐ
To Deliver	ܦܲܨܹܐ ܡܲܦܨܹܐ
Blossom	ܦܸܩܚܵܐ
Savior	ܦܵܪܘܿܩܵܐ
Saved	ܦܪܸܩ ܝܼܦܪܘܿܩ
S	ܨ
Will	ܨܸܒ݂ܝܵܢܵܐ
To Thirst	ܨܗܹܐ : ܝܼܨܗܹܐ

Fast	ܨܘܡܐ
Image / Picture	ܨܘܪܬܐ
Prayer	ܨܠܘܬܐ
Cross	ܨܠܝܒܐ
Image / Idol	ܨܠܡܐ
Bird	ܨܦܪܐ ܨܦܪܐ

Q ܩ

Holy	ܩܕܝܫܐ
Neck	ܩܕܠܐ
Monkey	ܩܘܦܐ
Killed	ܩܛܠ : ܩܛܝܠܐ
Wood	ܩܝܣܐ
Voice	ܩܠܐ
Priest / Elder	ܩܫܝܫܐ
Called	ܩܪܐ : ܩܪܝܐ

R ܪ

Big / Great / Large	ܪܒܐ
Leg / Foot	ܪܓܠܐ
Wind / Spirit	ܪܘܚܐ

Holy Spirit	ܪܘܚܐ ܕܩܘܕܫܐ
Friend	ܪܚܡܐ
High	ܪܡܐ
Evening	ܪܡܫܐ
Reconciled	ܪܥܝ ܡܪܥܝ
Head	ܪܫܐ
Sh	ܫ
Praised	ܫܒܚ: ܡܫܒܚ
Forgave	ܫܒܩ ܡܫܒܩ
Apostle	ܫܠܝܚܐ
Peace	ܫܠܡܐ
Name / Names	ܫܡܐ: ܫܡܗܐ
Sky / Heaven / Heavens	ܫܡܝܐ
Deacon	ܫܡܫܐ
Sun	ܫܡܫܐ
Beautiful	ܫܦܝܪܐ
Began	ܫܪܝ: ܡܫܪܐ
Truth	ܫܪܪܐ

T

ܬ

Thomas

ܬܐܘܡܐ

Came

ܬܹܐ ܕܹܐܬܹܐ

Bull

ܬܘܿܪܵܐ

Snow

ܬܲܠܓܵܐ

Student / Disciple

ܬܲܠܡܝܼܕܵܐ

Interpreted

ܬܲܪܓܸܡ : ܡܬܲܪܓܸܡ

Door

ܬܲܪܥܵܐ

Glory

ܬܸܫܒܘܿܚܬܵܐ

Service

ܬܸܫܡܸܫܬܵܐ

DICTIONARY
ENGLISH – ARAMAIC

A

Adam ܐܕܡ

Alive / Living ܚܝܐ

All ܟܠ

Also ܐܦ

Angel ܡܠܐܟܐ

Apostle ܫܠܝܚܐ

August ܐܒ

B

Baghdad ܒܓܕܕ

Bear ܕܒܐ

Beautiful ܫܦܝܪܐ

Behold ܗܐ

Began ܫܪܝ ܂ ܡܫܪܐ

Bell ܙܓܐ

Beloved ܚܒܝܒ

Big / Great / Large	ܪܲܒܵܐ
Bird	ܛܲܝܪܵܐ
Black	ܐܘܼܟ݂ܵܡܵܐ
Bless	ܒܲܪܸܟ݂
Blessing	ܒܘܼܪܟܵܬ݂ܵܐ
Blind	ܣܲܡܝܵܐ
Blood	ܕܸܡܵܐ
Blossom	ܦܸܩܚܵܐ
Bold	ܚܲܨܝܼܢܵܐ
Book	ܟܬ݂ܵܒ݂ܵܐ
Bone	ܓܲܪܡܵܐ
Bride	ܟܲܠܬ݂ܵܐ
Brother	ܐܲܚܵܐ
Bubble	ܚܒ݂ܵܒ݂ܵܐ
Built	ܒܢܵܐ : ܒܢܹܐ
But	ܐܝܼܢܵܐ

C

Called	ܩܪܹܐ
Camel	ܓܲܡܠܵܐ

Canal	ܚܒܬܐ
Cat	ܩܛܐ
Cave	ܟܦܐ
Chest	ܠܘܚܐ
Christ / Messiah	ܡܫܝܚܐ
Consoled	ܒܝܐ
Cook	ܒܫܠܐ
Created	ܚܕܐ ܒܪܐ
Cross	ܨܠܝܒܐ

D

Daughter / Daughters	(ܒܪܬܝ) ܒܪܬܐ : ܒܢܬܐ
Day	ܝܘܡܐ
Day (24 hrs.)	ܢܘܡܐ
Deacon	ܡܫܡܫܢܐ
Debt / Offense	ܚܘܒܐ
December	ܟܢܘܢ ܐ
Delicious	ܒܣܝܡܐ
Delivered	ܦܨܐ
Den / Well	ܓܘܒܐ

Destroyed	ܚܝܒ
Disciple / Student	ܬܠܡܝܕܐ
Dog	ܟܠܒܐ
Dream	ܚܠܡܐ
Drink	ܡܫܬܝܐ

E

Ear	ܐܕܢܐ
Earth	ܐܪܥܐ
Eat	ܐܟܠ : ܐܟܘܠ
Elephant	ܦܝܠܐ
Even as	ܐܝܟܢܐ
Evening	ܪܡܫܐ
Evil	ܒܝܫܐ
Eye	ܥܝܢܐ

F

Fast	ܨܘܡܐ
Fell	ܢܦܠ : ܢܦܘܠ
Fire	ܢܘܪܐ

Fish	ܢܘܢܐ
Fish egg	ܟܒܕܐ
Flower / Rose	ܘܪܕܐ
Forgave	ܫܒܩ ܝܥܩܘܒ
Foot / Leg	ܪܓܠܐ
Forever	ܠܥܠܡ
Fortune	ܓܕܐ
Friday	ܥܪܘܒܬܐ
Friend	ܪܚܡܐ
From	ܡܢ
Fruit	ܦܐܪܐ

G

Glory / Praise	ܫܘܒܚܐ
God	ܐܠܗܐ
Good	ܛܒܐ
Grace	ܛܝܒܘܬܐ
Gust / Hurricane	ܥܠܥܠܐ

H

Hand	ܐܝܼܕܵܐ
Happy / Delighted	ܚܲܕܘܼܬܵܐ
Harvest	ܚܨܵܕܵܐ
Head	ܪܹܫܵܐ
Heart	ܠܸܒܵܐ
Heaven / Heavens / Sky	ܫܡܲܝܵܐ
Holy	ܩܲܕܝܼܫܵܐ
Holy Spirit	ܪܘܼܚܵܐ ܕܩܘܼܕܫܵܐ
Horse / Mare	ܣܘܼܣܝܵܐ : ܣܘܼܣܬܵܐ
House / Houses	ܒܲܝܬܵܐ ܒܵܬܹ̈ܐ
Human being / Man	ܒܲܪܢܵܫܵܐ
Humble / Meek	ܡܲܟܝܼܟܵܐ
To Hunger	ܟܦܢ

I

Image / Idol	ܨܲܠܡܵܐ
Image / Picture	ܨܘܼܪܬܵܐ
To Inherit	ܝܪܬ
Inside	ܠܓܵܘ
Interpreted	ܦܫܝܼܩ

J

January	ܟܢܘܢ ܒ
Jaw	ܝܚܐ
Jesus	ܦܟܐ
John	ܝܫܘܥ
Jonah	ܝܘܚܢܢ
Joseph	ܝܘܢܢ
Judgment	ܝܘܣܦ
Justice / Goodness	ܕܝܢܐ
	ܛܒܘܬܐ

K

Killed	ܩܛܠ
King	ܡܠܟܐ

L

Laughed	ܓܚܟ
Let Come	ܬܐܬܐ
Let there be / Will be	ܢܗܘܐ
Life	ܚܝܐ
Linen cloth	ܟܬܢܐ
Lord / Sir	ܡܪܐ

195

Lord God	ܡܪܝܐ ܐܠܗܐ
Lost	ܐܒܝܕ ܒܐܒܝܕ
Love	ܚܘܒܐ
M	
Made / Did / Work	ܥܒܕ
Make joyful	ܚܕܝ
Man / Anyone / Person	ܐܢܫ
Mare	ܣܘܣܬܐ
Mark	ܡܪܩܘܣ
Martyr	ܣܗܕܐ
Mary / Miriam	ܡܪܝܡ
Merciful	ܚܢܢܐ
Milk	ܚܠܒܐ
Monkey	ܩܘܦܐ
Moon	ܣܗܪܐ
Mosquito	ܒܩܐ
Mother / Mothers	ܐܡܐ : ܐܡܗܬܐ
Mountain	ܛܘܪܐ
Mourner	ܐܒܝܠܐ

N

Neck	ܨܘܪܐ
Need	ܣܘܢܩܢܐ
No	ܠܐ
Nose	ܢܚܝܪܐ

O

On / Upon / Over / Above	ܥܠ

P

Began	ܫܪܝ : ܫܪܝܘ
Peace	ܫܠܡܐ
People	ܥܡܐ
Pious / Just / Kind	ܟܐܢܐ
Place	ܕܘܟܐ
Poor	ܡܣܟܢܐ
Pope	ܦܦܐ
Pure	ܕܟܝܐ
Praise / Glory	ܫܘܒܚܐ
Praised	ܫܒܚ : ܫܒܚܘ
Prayer	ܨܠܘܬܐ

197

Priest (Ancient temple priest	ܟܗܢܐ
Priest / Elder	ܩܫܝܫܐ
Prosperity	ܚܘܣܢܐ

Q

Queen / Queens	ܡܠܟܬܐ : ܡܠܟܬܐ

R

Rabbit	ܐܪܢܒܐ
Reconciled	ܪܥܝ
Red	ܣܘܡܩܐ
Rest	ܢܝܚܐ
Reward	ܐܓܪܐ
Righteous	ܘܕܝܩܐ

S

Said	ܐܡܪ ܐܡܪ
Salt	ܡܠܚܐ
Satisfied	ܣܒܥ
Saved	ܦܪܩ ܦܪܩܘܢ
Savior	ܦܪܘܩܐ

Saw	ܡܣܪܐ ܝܣܘܥ
Sea	ܝܡܐ
Service	ܬܫܡܫܬܐ
Skin	ܡܫܟܐ
Side	ܓܒܐ
Simon Peter	ܫܡܥܘܢ ܟܐܦܐ
Sin	ܚܛܝܬܐ
Small (Little)	ܙܥܘܪܐ
Snow	ܬܠܓܐ
Son / Sons	ܒܪܐ : ܒܢܝܐ
Spear	ܡܘܪܢܝܬܐ
Spirit	ܪܘܚܐ
Star	ܟܘܟܒܐ
Sun	ܫܡܫܐ

T

Teacher	ܡܠܦܢܐ
Temple	ܗܝܟܠܐ
Temptation	ܢܣܝܘܢܐ

There is / are / to be	ܐܝܬ
There is no / are none / will not be	ܠܝܬ
Thief	ܓܢܒܐ
To Thirst	ܨܗܝ
Thomas	ܬܐܘܡܐ
Thorn	ܟܘܒܐ
Time	ܙܒܢܐ
Toward / With / To	ܠܘܬ
Track	ܥܩܒܐ
Treasure	ܓܙܐ
Tree	ܐܝܠܢܐ
Truth	ܫܪܪܐ

V

Virgin / Virgins	ܒܬܘܠܐ ܒܬܘܠܬܐ
Voice	ܩܠܐ

W

Walked	ܗܠܟ
Wall	ܐܣܬܐ
Wart	ܥܩܣܐ
Way	ܐܘܪܚܐ

200

Wedding	ܣܠܘܿܟܵܐ
Went	ܙܸܠܹܗ
What	ܡܵܢܝܼ
White	ܚܸܘܵܪܵܐ
Will	ܒܸܕ ܗܵܘܹܐ
Wind	ܦܘܿܚܵܐ
Wise	ܚܲܟܝܼܡܵܐ
Wisdom	ܚܸܟܡܬܵܐ
With	ܥܲܡ
Wolf	ܕܹܐܒ݂ܵܐ
Woman / Wife / Women	ܒܲܟ݂ܬܵܐ (ܢܸܫܹ̈ܐ)
Wood	ܩܲܝܣܵܐ
Word / Words	ܗܹܡܸܙܡܵܢ : ܡܸܠܬܵܐ
World	ܥܵܠܡܵܐ
Wrote	ܟܬܸܒ݂ܠܹܗ

ABOUT THE AUTHORS

ABOUT THE AUTHOR

Michael J. Bazzi

The Rev. Fr. Michael J. Bazzi (emeritus), L.S.T., has been the pastor of St. Peter's Chaldean Catholic Church in El Cajon, San Diego, since 1985. Fr. Michael has also served as a professor of modern and classical Aramaic at Cuyamaca College in El Cajon from 1989 to 2020. Fr. Michael is a distinguished Bible authority, author, teacher, linguist, translator, and pastoral counselor.

Born in Tilkepe, Iraq, a suburb of Nineveh, he graduated seminary at St. Peter's College, Baghdad, and was ordained into the priesthood in that same year, 1964. He served eight years in Tilkepe, assisting as a priest, speaking his native language of Aramaic, as well as Arabic. He then travelled to the Vatican in Rome where he earned a Master's Degree in Pastoral Theology. While in Italy he gained a broad knowledge of the Italian and French languages.

Fr. Michael arrived in Oshkosh — Green Bay, Wisconsin in 1974. Here he taught and preached Scripture from the Aramaic point of view. Later, he established parishes in Oak Park and Troy, Michigan, and in 1983-85, served in Los Angeles, California. Fr. Michael moved to San Diego in 1985. In 1987, he became pastor of St. Peters Church in El Cajon, where he is now pastor emeritus.

Fr. Michael was the San Diego Law Enforcement Association's Citizen of the Year in 2010.

Books by Fr. Michael J. Bazzi available at:
www.Letinthelightpublishing.com:

1. *Tilkepe*
2. *The Life of Tilkpenaye*
3. *Classical Aramaic I &II*
4. *Modern Aramaic Vol. I & II*
5. *Beginners Handbook of the Aramaic Language*
6. *Read and Write Aramaic (for children)*
7. *Know your Faith*
8. *Who are the Chaldeans?*
9. *Teach yourself the Bible: Pentateuch & Matthew*
10. *Chaldean Nation*

ABOUT THE AUTHOR

Rocco A. Errico

Dr. Rocco A. Errico is an ordained minister, international lecturer and author, spiritual counselor, and one of the nation's leading Bible scholars working from the original Aramaic Peshitta texts. For ten years, he studied intensively with Dr. George M. Lamsa, Th. D., (1890-1975), world renowned Assyrian biblical scholar and translator of the Holy Bible from the Ancient Eastern Text. Dr. Errico is proficient in Aramaic and Hebrew exegesis, helping thousands of readers and seminar participant understand how the Semitic context of culture, language, idioms, symbolism, mystical style, psychology, and literary amplification- the Seven Keys that unlock the Bible- are essential to understanding the ancient spiritual document.

Dr. Errico is the recipient of numerous awards and academic degrees, including a Doctorate in Philosophy from the School of Christianity in Los Angeles; a Doctorate in Divinity from St. Ephrem's Institute in Sweden; and a Doctorate in Sacred Theology from the School of Christianity in Los Angeles. In 1993, the American Apostolic University College of Seminarians awarded him a Doctorate of Letters. He. Also holds a special title of Teacher, Prime Exegete, Maplana d'miltha dalaha, among the Federation of St. Thomas Christians of the Order of Antioch. In 2002, Dr. Errico was inducted into the Morehouse College Collegium of Scholars.

Dr. Errico is a featured speaker at conferences, symposia, and seminars throughout the United States, Canada, Mexico, and Europe. Dr. Errico has been a regular contributor for over 35 years to *Science of Mind Magazine* a monthly journal founded in 1927. He began his practice as an ordained minister and pastoral counselor in the mid-1950's and during the next three decades served in churches and missions in Missouri, Texas, New Mexico, and California. Throughout his public work, Dr. Errico has stressed the nonsectarian, open interpretation of Biblical spirituality, prying it free from 2000 years of rigid orthodoxy, which, according to his research, is founded on incorrect translations of the Aramaic texts.

In 1970, Dr. Errico established the Noohra Foundation in San Antonio, Texas, as a non-profit, non-sectarian spiritual educational organization devoted tp helping people of all faiths to understand the Near Eastern background and Aramaic interpretations of the Bible. In 1976, Dr. Errico relocated the Noohra Foundation in Irvine, California, where it flourished for the next 17 years. For seven years, the Noohra Foundation operated in Santa Fe, New Mexico, and in September 2001, it relocated to Smyrna, Georgia, where Dr. Errico served as Dean of Biblical Studies for Dr. Barbara King's School of Ministry Hillside Chapel and Truth Center in Atlanta.

Under the auspices of the Noohra Foundation, Dr. Errico continues to lecture for colleges, civic group and churches of various denominations in the United States, Canada, Mexico and Europe.

Books by Dr. Errico

1. *Aramaic Light on the Beatitudes*
2. *Let There Be Light: The Seven Keys*
3. *And There Was Light*
4. *Setting a Trap for God: The Aramaic Prayer of Jesus*
5. *The Mysteries of Creation: The Genesis Story*
6. *The Message of Mathew: An Annotated Parallel Aramaic - English Gospel of Mathew*
7. *La Antigua Oracion Aramea De Jesus: El Padrenuestro*
8. *Das Aramaische Vaterunser*
9. *Es Werde Licht*
10. *Otto Accordi Con Dio: il Padre Nostro orginario*

Commentaries by Dr. Rocco A. Errico and Dr. George M Lamsa:

Aramaic Light on the Gospel of Mathew, Aramaic Light on the Gospels of Mark and Luke, Aramaic Light on the Gospel of John, Aramaic Light on the Acts of the Apostles, Aramaic Light on Romans Through 2 Corinthians, Aramaic Light on Galatians Through Hebrews, Aramaic Light on James

Through Revelation, Aramaic Light on Genesis, Aramaic Light on Exodus Through Deuteronomy, Aramaic Light on Joshua Through 2 Chronicles, Aramaic Light on Ezra Through the Song of Solomon, and *Aramaic Light on Isaiah, Jeremiah, and Lamentations, Aramaic Light on Ezekiel, Daniel, and the Minor Prophets.*

To order these and other books, or if you are interested in contacting Dr. Errico about a personal appearance, please contact:

Noohra Foundation
PMB 343
4480 South Cobb Dr. SE Ste. H
Smyrna, GA 30080

www.noohra.com
Phone: 678-260-5021

Notes

Notes

Typesetting and printing at Venus Printing
San Diego, CA / 2025 / Tel: 619.590.1148
E. Mail: info@venusprinting.com
1183 E. Main St., Ste. D, El Cajon, CA 92021

www.ingramcontent.com/pod-product-compliance
Lightning Source LLC
Chambersburg PA
CBHW080804300426
44114CB00020B/2827